HOMEMADE
RAVIOLI
MADE SIMPLE

C000060396

HOMEMADE RAVIOLI MADE SIMPLE

50 Mix-and-Match Recipes for the Best Filled Pastas

CARMELLA ALVARO

Photography by Hélène Dujardin

ROCKRIDGE PRESS

Copyright © 2021 by Rockridge Press, Emeryville, California

No part of this publication may be reproduced, stored in a retrieval system, or transmitted in any form or by any means, electronic, mechanical, photocopying, recording, scanning, or otherwise, except as permitted under Sections 107 or 108 of the 1976 United States Copyright Act, without the prior written permission of the Publisher. Requests to the Publisher for permission should be addressed to the Permissions Department, Rockridge Press, 6005 Shellmound Street, Suite 175, Emeryville, CA 94608.

Limit of Liability/Disclaimer of Warranty: The Publisher and the author make no representations or warranties with respect to the accuracy or completeness of the contents of this work and specifically disclaim all warranties, including without limitation warranties of fitness for a particular purpose. No warranty may be created or extended by sales or promotional materials. The advice and strategies contained herein may not be suitable for every situation. This work is sold with the understanding that the Publisher is not engaged in rendering medical, legal, or other professional advice or services. If professional assistance is required, the services of a competent professional person should be sought. Neither the Publisher nor the author shall be liable for damages arising herefrom. The fact that an individual, organization, or website is referred to in this work as a citation and/or potential source of further information does not mean that the author or the Publisher endorses the information the individual, organization, or

website may provide or recommendations they/it may make. Further, readers should be aware that websites listed in this work may have changed or disappeared between when this work was written and when it is read.

For general information on our other products and services or to obtain technical support, please contact our Customer Care Department within the United States at (866) 744-2665, or outside the United States at (510) 253-0500.

Rockridge Press publishes its books in a variety of electronic and print formats. Some content that appears in print may not be available in electronic books, and vice versa.

TRADEMARKS: Rockridge Press and the Rockridge Press logo are trademarks or registered trademarks of Callisto Media Inc. and/or its affiliates, in the United States and other countries, and may not be used without written permission. All other trademarks are the property of their respective owners. Rockridge Press is not associated with any product or vendor mentioned in this book.

Interior and Cover Designer: Brian Lewis
Art Producer: Sara Feinstein
Editor: Anne Goldberg
Production Manager: Holly Haydash

Photography © 2021 Hélène Dujardin. Food styling by Anna Hamptom. Author photo courtesy of Sara Davis.

Paperback ISBN: 978-1-63807-122-8
eBook ISBN: 978-1-63807-172-3
R0

To my husband and official taste tester, Billy, who supports me with infinite patience and love in everything I do.

CONTENTS

QUADRUCCI, MEZZELUNE, SACCHETTINI, DOPPIO RAVIOLI,
TORTELLINI, RAVIOLI, LUNE, AGNOLOTTI, TRIANGLES

INTRODUCTION

I first learned to make pasta by hand in one of the Italian cities that claims the supremacy of stuffed pasta—Bologna. I watched in amazement as the *sfogline* (Italian pasta makers in aprons and poufy white hats) rolled out giant sheets of pasta by hand to make the tiny, round, meat-filled tortellini the city is known for. They cut the sheets into 1-inch squares, dabbed some filling in one corner, and sealed and twisted the pasta to form hundreds of perfectly shaped tortellini, which were immediately brought downstairs to the pasta shop to be sold by the kilo for someone to enjoy for dinner that very night.

After that experience, I knew my corporate career was over and that my Italian vacation had turned me toward a new vocation: pasta maker. I came home from Italy, immediately started making fresh stuffed pasta to sell at the farmers' market, and founded Melina's Fresh Pasta. Eleven years later, we are still feeding ravioli to our fans in and around Durham, North Carolina.

The simplest stuffed pasta is a filling made of vegetables, meat, cheese, or fruit sealed inside pasta dough. But Italians don't make food simple. There are so many names, shapes, sizes, fillings, and sauces that it would make a roomful of *nonnas* dizzy. It is my hope that this book will be a useful guide to the many varieties of stuffed pastas and flavors found all over Italy. Whether you're new to pasta making or just looking for new stuffed pasta recipes to satisfy your cravings, the following pages explain in detail the process of making stuffed pastas, so you can create your own agnolotti, ravioli, tortellini, and more at home.

This book begins with a short history and explanation of stuffed pasta. First, I discuss pasta dough making and review the tools you will need to make stuffed pasta in your kitchen. Then comes the fun part: 50 recipes for doughs, fillings, and sauces. The five dough recipes can be mixed and matched with the 30 different filling recipes and topped with your choice of 15 sauces (plus a few more simple sauce recipes included within the stuffed pasta recipes in chapter 3). Although there is a focus on remaking classic and traditional Italian recipes, I also include some of my favorite fillings that use Italian ingredients with a twist.

Let's put on our aprons (poufy white hat optional), channel our inner nonna, or nonno, and start stuffing some pasta!

CHAPTER ONE.

RAVIOLI AT HOME

IN ITALY, THERE are as many recipes for stuffed pasta as there are nonnas; every region, town, and house has a different name, spelling, recipe, filling, shape, and style for their stuffed pasta. Because these pastas can, sometimes, be labor intensive and use rich ingredients, Italians make and eat stuffed pasta at home mostly on religious feast days, weddings, and holidays, especially Christmas.

And although there is a bit of effort required to make stuffed pasta, this book helps simplify the process and makes it possible for you to make stuffed pasta at home. In this chapter, you'll learn about the different types of stuffed pasta, and I'll show you how to mix and match doughs, fillings, and sauces to create your own delicious masterpieces in your home kitchen.

A Stuffed Pasta Bonanza

Every region in Italy takes credit for inventing stuffed pasta. Rich ingredients wrapped in pasta dough was originally the food of the wealthy, made by chefs to serve at lavish banquets. The earliest accounts of ravioli can be found around the fourteenth century, and early stuffed pasta fillings included esoteric ingredients such as brains. Luckily, stuffed pasta made its way into humbler kitchens in the style of *cucina povera* ("poor kitchen") or peasant cooking, which involves using a few simple, fresh, local ingredients to make hearty meals. Pasta fillings are made with ingredients such as cheeses, vegetables, or leftover meats, and the stuffed pasta is cooked in broth or topped with a simple sauce.

While researching for this book, I found that Italian food is as delicious as it is exhausting. There is little agreement on fillings, ingredients, shapes, and sizes for stuffed pasta—every family has their own recipe that has been passed down through generations. This type of pasta can be called anything from agnolotti or cappellacci to ravioli or tortelli. It can be shaped into circles or squares, twisted into little rings, folded into half-moons, and more. The filling can be traditional, like spinach and cheese, regionally based, like pumpkin, or comprise any flavor combination that catches an Italian's fancy that day. There are so many types of stuffed pasta that vary across regions—even from house to house—that I found it challenging to narrow down the recipe list.

For this book, I define *stuffed pasta* as pasta dough wrapped around a filling made of any combination of meats, cheeses, vegetables, and fruits and fully sealed (sorry, manicotti). The particular stuffed pasta can have different names based on its shape or size, with the most common being called ravioli or tortelli. I do my best to explain the traditional name, size, filling, and shape when applicable.

In the pages to come, you will find 50 recipes for pasta doughs, fillings, and sauces. For some recipes, I followed tradition closely because I don't want to cross an Italian nonna. (They are surprisingly strong and lethal with wooden spoons.) Other recipes reflect what I do at Melina's Fresh Pasta Shop: I find flavors I like, combine them, and stuff them into pasta dough. Because I cannot survey every Italian—and many wouldn't share their secret family recipes with me, even if I begged—I chose recipes that offer a wide variety of options that can be mixed and matched based on personal tastes. Regardless of the pasta's name or shape, I promise you these recipes are delicious.

A Pasta Maker's Kitchen

Before we begin the pasta-making process, I will introduce the staple ingredients and equipment needed to create the recipes in this book.

BASIC TOOLS

These essential tools make the process of homemade pasta easier and more efficient.

Baking sheets: Baking sheets dusted with flour are used to help store your stuffed pastas until you are ready to cook them. You can also use these pans to freeze pasta.

Bench scraper: This simple tool is used to make dough and clean your pasta board. It can also be used to cut dough.

Knife: A sharp knife will help you cut the shapes needed to form stuffed pasta.

Pasta roller/machine: This hand-operated, tabletop pasta machine attaches to a counter and simplifies the stuffed pasta-making process. It produces a more consistent sheet of dough than you can achieve with a rolling pin. The machines come with both rollers and cutters, but for stuffed pasta, you just need the smooth roller to make a pasta sheet. (I recommend the Marcato brand.)

Plastic wrap: Plastic wrap keeps the dough from drying out while it rests or until it's rolled out. Tightly wrap the completed dough ball in plastic anytime it is not being used.

Rolling pin: In the absence of a mechanical roller, a rolling pin, or *mattarello*, can be used to thin the dough. It is also helpful to use with a ravioli mold (see page 4) to seal and cut the pasta. Best results come from using a pin made from a solid piece of wood, about 3 feet long, to roll pasta dough.

Skimmer/slotted spoon: Stuffed pasta is delicate, and I do not recommend dumping the pasta into a colander to strain it after cooking because the pasta might tear open, releasing the filling. Instead, use a slotted spoon or skimmer, which has a long handle with a shallow mesh or wire basket at the end, to gently remove the pasta from the cooking water.

Wood pasta (or cutting) board: A large wooden surface is necessary to make pasta dough. You can use an oversized cutting board or a specially made pasta board. You don't need a custom board; buy a 2-by-4-foot piece of precut, untreated wood from the hardware store to use for this purpose.

SPECIALTY ITEMS

If you are going to make stuffed pasta regularly, I recommend some of the equipment listed below to up your stuffed pasta–making game.

Fluted/crinkle-edged pastry cutter: A fluted pastry cutter creates a pretty, wavy edge on your stuffed pasta, as opposed to the sharp, even edge of a knife cut. I recommend a pastry cutter with two wheels—a smooth cutter to cut shapes and a fluted wheel to cut and seal more decorative edges.

Food processor: A food processor is useful throughout the stuffed pasta-making process for making doughs, pureeing sauces, and blending fillings. Instead of hand chopping and mixing, use a food processor to save time and make more consistent pasta fillings and sauces.

Pastry/piping bag or zip-top bag: It is helpful to use a pastry bag to pipe the filling onto the pasta dough. Piping the filling through the pastry bag, or through a snipped corner of a zip-top bag, is a more precise and consistent method than spooning the filling onto the dough.

Ravioli mold: A ravioli mold produces beautiful, uniform ravioli by the dozens in much less time than it takes to form each ravioli individually. These small trays with 10 to 12 spaces for ravioli also include a press and, sometimes, a small rolling pin. Look for a tray with holes rather than indentations in the metal because they are easier to use than solid trays are, and they prevent the dough from sticking to the mold. I recommend using these molds anytime you're making stuffed pasta for a crowd.

Ravioli press/stamps: There are many shapes and sizes of ravioli stamps available. The stamps usually come with a wooden handle attached to a metal cutter. These tools give you uniform shapes when making and sealing individual ravioli. In a pinch, you can also use a cookie cutter, the open end of a drinking glass, or even a bottle cap (see page 68) to seal and cut ravioli.

Stand mixer and roller attachment: If you prefer not to use your hands to make pasta dough, it can be made with a food processor or a stand mixer. The pasta roller attachment that comes with a stand mixer really helps speed up the pasta-making process, too. Instead of using a rolling pin, this automated roller helps you transform dough into sheets of pasta ready for stuffing in no time and with little effort.

～ THE KITCHEN SCALE ～

Making pasta dough isn't as exacting a process as baking bread or making French pastry, but it is helpful to use a kitchen scale to weigh flour, and sometimes even liquids, to eliminate the guesswork from dough making. Although there will always be an element of "feel" to making pasta dough, using a scale gives you a consistent amount of base ingredients to work with each time you make pasta. Weighing ingredients also allows you to accurately scale recipes up or down, depending on how much pasta you want to make. A scale is also helpful for sauce and filling ingredients, when more exact measurements are required to get just the right flavors.

INGREDIENTS

Listed here are the most common ingredients needed to make pasta doughs, fillings, and sauces. Italian cooking generally requires just a few ingredients, so they need to be the freshest possible and of the highest quality.

Flour

Many different flours can be used to make pasta doughs. Here are some of the most common:

Tipo "00" or double zero flour: With its fine, powdery consistency, this is the traditional flour used to make pasta dough. Combined with eggs, it produces a soft, pliable dough that seals well. It is commonly available and can be found in most specialty grocery stores or online.

All-purpose flour: This flour type is a good substitute when you don't have Tipo "00" flour. A pasta dough made with all-purpose flour won't be quite as soft as one made with "00" flour, because all-purpose flour is less finely milled, but all-purpose flour can be used interchangeably with Tipo "00" for pasta dough with good results, either with water or eggs.

Whole wheat flour: This flour is speckled brown because it contains parts of the wheat berry (the bran, germ, and endosperm), and it has a nuttier flavor than all-purpose flour. A little more egg or water is needed when making pasta dough with whole wheat flour because it absorbs more liquid.

Gluten-free flour: When using gluten-free flour for pasta, you will need to add a stabilizer, such as xanthan gum, to form a dough that will hold together for pasta. There are gluten-free flour blends available, such as Cup4Cup and King Arthur's Measure for Measure, which include stabilizers and are 1:1 substitutes for wheat flour, so all you need to do is mix the flour with eggs to make pasta dough.

Eggs

Eggs add fat and protein to pasta dough, which help the pasta hold its shape. Protein also affects gluten formation, which makes the dough easier to shape. Eggs also help bind fillings, especially meat, but I only add eggs to fillings that don't have ricotta, because ricotta is a good binder, too. *Eggs should be at room temperature* for making pasta dough, so remember to take them out of the refrigerator about 45 minutes before you'll need them. Visit your local farmers' market to find the freshest eggs possible.

Salt

I do not add salt to my pasta dough, but salt is needed to season fillings and sauces and is important for cooking pasta. For fillings and sauces, salt can be adjusted to taste unless a specific amount is indicated in a recipe. Some recipes indicate that the filling ingredients have enough salt, so no added salt is needed.

Water

Water for making pasta dough should be at room temperature. Refer to the sidebar on page 8 to learn about water's role in sauce making.

It is essential to add salt to pasta cooking water, because that is the only time the pasta itself is seasoned. The pasta water should be salted generously. I use a healthy handful, but if you want to measure the amount, use 1 to 2 tablespoons of kosher salt per 4 quarts of cooking water. Try cooking pasta in unsalted and salted water to taste the difference.

Olive oil and butter

I always use extra-virgin olive oil when cooking. I don't use the most expensive, fruitiest olive oil that I would use for dressings or dipping, but I do try to use a high-quality extra-virgin olive oil. I also use salted butter and adjust the salt in the finished dish to account for it.

Sauce Ingredients

Cream, meat, and pesto sauces should always be made with fresh, high-quality ingredients.

Cream sauces and sauces with cheese: When making a prepared sauce, versus using reserved pasta cooking water to make a quick pan sauce, you'll need heavy cream to create the right texture. When using cheese for sauce, it is best to grate or shred the cheese yourself to avoid the anti-clumping additives in pre-shredded cheese. Grating will give you a smoother sauce.

Non-tomato-based sauces: Although you can substitute any type of herb or green in pesto sauce to your preference, always use fresh, not dried. Lemons need to be freshly zested and juiced. For sauces that call for ground meat, I use 90/10 ground beef, which eliminates having to drain off excess fat and results in a less oily sauce.

Tomato-based sauces: Italians usually have a pantry ingredient called "passata" on hand—uncooked tomatoes that have been pureed and then strained, with no additives, either bottled or homemade—which they use as a base for all tomato sauces. I substitute canned crushed tomatoes for passata in my recipes because they are more readily available. When whole tomatoes are specified, use either fresh plum tomatoes or canned whole "San Marzano-style" tomatoes. San Marzano tomatoes are less acidic than other tomatoes and are perfect for sauces.

Filling Ingredients

Fillings can be made of meat, vegetables, beans, cheese, and fruit in any combination. The basic formula I use for fillings is to blend a ricotta cheese base with flavorful ingredients (such as meat or vegetables, cooked or raw). Some recipes eliminate cheese for a dairy-free alternative. Many vegetable-based fillings use raw vegetables, eliminating cooking and straining to remove extra liquid. Meat fillings without ricotta require an egg to bind them.

Cheese

Whole milk ricotta is the base of many fillings in this book. I also use Pecorino Romano and Parmesan cheeses interchangeably for fillings, sauces, and garnishes. I prefer Pecorino Romano for its sharper, saltier flavor, but in some recipes, Parmesan's more delicate flavor is appropriate.

THE MAGIC OF PASTA WATER

Don't dump pasta cooking water down the drain! That starchy liquid becomes an essential ingredient to thicken sauces and help the sauce cling to the pasta without using cream or other ingredients, and it adds a bit of salt to the dish (because you remembered to salt your pasta cooking water, of course). That's why I do not dump my pasta into a colander after it's done cooking; I always remove the pasta from the cooking water using a skimmer or slotted spoon. Then, the pasta water stays in the pot, waiting to be used. A few tablespoons, or up to 1 cup or more, of the cooking water is usually called for to finish quick sauces.

Stuffed Pasta Techniques

Once you master a few critical pasta-making steps, you will be rolling out dough and pinching together stuffed pasta as fast as any native Italian. Using the right tools and techniques will help you master pasta dough and shaping.

Here, we will focus on mixing pasta dough by hand, which is the best way to learn how to get the right texture and feel for the pasta dough. You'll also find instructions for mixing pasta dough using either a food processor or stand mixer on page 21, following the recipe for Traditional Egg Pasta Dough, which can be applied to most dough recipes in this book.

STEP 1: MIXING THE DOUGH

1. Place the flour on a cutting board or pasta board. Make a wide, shallow well in the center of the flour. This should look like a ring of flour with a bare center that goes all the way down to the wood, creating a barrier to hold the eggs.

2. Place the cracked eggs in the center of the well. Using a fork, gently beat the eggs in the center of the well until the yolks and whites are thoroughly blended, being careful not to let the eggs overflow the walls of the flour well.

3. Use the fork to pull some of the flour from the inside walls of the well into the egg mixture. Mix until the flour is absorbed by the eggs. Repeat, gradually adding flour and beating it into the egg, until the dough begins to look shaggy.

4. Use a bench scraper to combine the remaining flour from the ring into the shaggy dough. Slide the scraper under the shaggy dough and flip it multiple times, folding over and over until the flour and eggs come together into a solid lump and there is not a lot of flour left that isn't incorporated. The dough will be dry at this point.

5. Using your hands, gather the dough into a ball and set it aside. Then, use the bench scraper to scrape the pasta board clean of dried dough and discard these bits.

STEP 2: KNEADING THE DOUGH

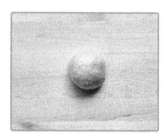

1. On the same (now clean) board, knead the dough ball: Using the heel of your hand and firm pressure, push and stretch the dough down and away from you at the same time, being careful not to smash the dough straight down into the board. You are stretching the dough, not trying to flatten it.

2. Rotate the dough a quarter turn, fold it in half, and repeat, pushing the dough firmly down and away. Continue kneading in this manner for no more than 10 minutes; any longer and the dough may dry out. As you continue to knead, the dough will start to look pale yellow and become elastic.

3. To determine when the dough is ready, test it by gently pressing on it with your finger. It should spring back easily, which means the dough is ready to rest. If the dough is still too soft and doesn't spring back, continue to knead and test until it does.

STEP 3: RESTING THE DOUGH

1. Wrap the dough tightly in plastic wrap, making sure to remove all the air so the dough doesn't dry out.

2. Let the dough rest at room temperature for about 30 minutes. (Do not refrigerate the dough.) During this time, the gluten formed during kneading begins to relax, which helps make the dough easier to roll into sheets or shapes. The dough will lose some of its springiness as it rests.

There are some common frustrations you may encounter when making fresh pasta dough, but they can be easily remedied. The most common issues are that the dough is too wet or too dry. Pasta making is sometimes more art than science, and the more you practice, the more you will get a feel for how the dough will behave under different conditions.

1. The dough is sticking to everything.

DO

→ When kneading, add 1 tablespoon of flour at a time until the dough stops sticking to your hands or the pasta board or rollers.

→ Rub flour on each side of the dough sheet if it sticks to the rolling pin or rollers. Thinning out the dough pushes out water and makes the pasta sticky as it thins.

→ Pay attention to the weather. A more humid day or climate will result in a wetter dough, so you may need to add more flour to balance this. Start with the standard ratio of liquid to flour and add more flour as needed; it is always easier to add more flour to fix a wet dough than to try to rehydrate a dry dough.

DON'T

→ It will be impossible to roll out the dough when it sticks to the rolling pin or pasta machine roller. Don't continue to try to roll it without rubbing more flour onto both sides of the dough.

2. The dough is too dry or won't hold together.

DO

→ When kneading, add a little more liquid by wetting your hands and continuing to knead the dough. Repeat until enough extra liquid is absorbed by the dough and the dough becomes more pliable.

→

→ When resting, dough will become dry when exposed to air, so always keep your dough tightly wrapped in plastic wrap when not using it.

→ When shaping and sealing, if the pasta is too dry and won't seal, rub a little water onto the edges of the shapes to seal the pasta around the filling.

·· DON'T ··

→ When shaping pasta, don't leave the extra pasta sheets or cut pieces exposed to air for too long. Cover any dough you're not using with a towel or plastic wrap while you are shaping other pieces.

STEP 4: ROLLING OUT THE DOUGH

You can use a pasta machine, stand mixer roller attachment, or rolling pin to thin your pasta dough.

Using a Pasta Machine or Stand Mixer Attachment

1. Pull the adjustment knob on the side of the roller to turn and adjust the roller to the widest setting (usually 1 or 0).

2. Remove one-fourth of the rested dough from the plastic, and rewrap the remaining dough. Form the small dough portion into a rectangle about the size of a deck of cards, about ¼ inch thick.

3. To help wake up the gluten after resting, feed the dough through the widest roller setting a few times, folding the dough in half each time

before sending it back through the roller. **Do not adjust the thickness of the roller until step 4.** You are using the rollers to knead the dough at this stage, not to thin it. Repeat feeding the dough through the roller at the widest setting until the dough can be stretched gently with your hands without tearing, usually three to four times. Test the dough by trying to gently pull it apart at the ends—when it stretches and doesn't tear, it is ready to thin out.

4. Now, begin to thin the dough by adjusting the pasta machine rollers and turning the dial up one number each time you feed the dough through the rollers. You may need to rub flour on both sides of the dough sheet between steps if it starts to stick to the rollers.

5. Continue to thread the sheet through the rollers, progressively adjusting the setting thinner and thinner. Thin the sheet until you can just start to see your fingers through the dough. For stuffed pasta, I like to thin the dough to setting number 5 or 6 on the pasta roller (a little thicker than for other pasta types).

Using a Rolling Pin

1. Dust the pasta board with flour, unwrap the dough ball, and place it on the floured board. Flatten the dough into a disk about 1 inch thick.

2. Start by rolling the pin across the dough, repeatedly pushing the pin away from you. Turn the dough a quarter turn periodically, and continue rolling and turning until the dough begins to thin out. If the dough sticks to the board or the pin, rub some additional flour on the dough.

3. Next, stretch the dough. Wrap three-fourths of the dough around the rolling pin, and let the remaining dough catch and hang off the edge of the pasta board in front of you. Stretch the dough by pushing the wrapped pin away from you on the pasta board. You are stretching the dough away from the flap hanging off the edge of the board, which thins the dough. Unfurl the dough from the pin and repeat this step, turning the dough a quarter turn each time before rolling and stretching.

4. Continue rolling: Lay the pasta sheet flat on the board, then roll the dough away from you; rotate the dough a quarter turn and repeat rolling three more times.

5. Repeat steps 3 and 4 until the dough is thin enough that you can just see your hand through it.

STEP 5: FILLING THE PASTA

Using a pastry bag to pipe fillings directly onto the pasta is recommended over scooping the filling onto the dough with spoons (measuring spoons work best, if this is the method you choose); the filling will be more consistent in amount and shape. You can also scoop the filling into a zip-top bag and snip off a bottom corner if you do not have a pastry bag.

How you space the filling on the dough for stuffed pasta will depend on the shape and size of your final rolled-out pasta sheet. With more practice, you will be able to roll out a neat rectangular sheet of dough. Before placing your filling on the bottom dough sheet, it helps to map out where to place the filling to ensure you have enough room to seal and cut the dough between each shape. You can do this with little dabs of filling, or you can make light indentations with a stamp across the sheet of dough. This will help you center the filling inside the stamp's area.

STEP 6: SHAPING, CUTTING, AND SEALING THE DOUGH

Each pasta shape will have its own technique to form, cut, and seal it. In order of ease, when forming basic shapes:

1. Use a knife or pastry cutter to cut the dough into shapes and your fingers to seal the edges securely.

2. Use a stamp, centered over the filling, to cut and seal one pasta shape at a time.

3. Use a mold, press, and rolling pin to seal and cut multiple uniform ravioli at a time.

   To offer as many options as possible for shaping pasta, each recipe in this book describes the specific method of cutting and shaping the dough (knife, stamp, or mold), but use whichever method you prefer once you master the recipe, depending on the tools you have on hand.

STEP 7: COOKING THE FILLED PASTA

Stuffed fresh pasta cooks quickly, usually in 4 to 5 minutes in boiling salted water. Because stuffed pasta freezes well, you can also cook it directly from frozen without thawing it first. Add 2 to 3 minutes of cooking time for frozen stuffed pastas.

   Stuffed pasta is delicate and prone to popping open and losing its filling. Once the water boils, gently place the pasta in the pot using a skimmer or slotted spoon. When all of the pasta has been added to the pot, gently stir it to make sure none of the pieces are sticking to the bottom of the pot. When finished cooking, do not dump cooked stuffed pasta into a colander to strain it, because the pasta may burst; instead, gently remove the pasta from the cooking water using the skimmer or slotted spoon you used to lower it into the water.

STEP 8: STORING THE PASTA

Filled fresh pastas have a shorter shelf life than freshly cut pasta. If you are not cooking the stuffed pasta immediately, refrigerate it and cook it within one day. Because the hand-rolled dough is thin, the filling will begin to leach into the dough, making it gummy and sticky. Freezing stuffed pasta right away is the best storage method. To freeze the pasta:

1. Arrange the pasta on a baking sheet lined with parchment paper in a single layer so the pieces do not touch. Place the baking sheet with the pasta in the freezer for 24 hours.

2. Remove the baking sheet and place the frozen pasta in resealable freezer-safe bags, removing as much air as possible before sealing the bags.

3. Place the bags in the freezer, where the frozen pasta will last for up to 6 months.

About the Recipes

Although making stuffed pasta does require a few steps and some time to get it right, these recipes were designed to be as clear, easy to follow, accessible, and inspiring as possible for every cook—not to mention delicious. Whether you're new to making stuffed pasta, have experience in the kitchen but want to learn more authentic pasta techniques, or are just searching for new recipes and techniques to try, there is something here for you.

Some filling and sauce recipes are as easy as blending ingredients in a food processor. Others require more cooking time and can be tackled as rainy-day projects or for special celebration meals and holidays. And, although some recipes may seem like they require hours of prep time, this time is usually hands-off cooking time with just some occasional stirring required.

Shaping stuffed pasta takes practice, and you might have some fails at first. There are a variety of shapes included in this book—from cutting simple squares to wrapping tortellini. Some recipes have more steps than others, but as long as the pasta is fully sealed around the filling, it will taste great, even if it doesn't look perfect. Although each recipe describes a specific way to shape the pasta, use whichever shaping method you prefer.

CHAPTER TWO

DOUGHS

IN THIS CHAPTER, there are five dough recipes that provide a lot of different options for the bases of your stuffed pasta creations, as well as satisfy any dietary requirements you may have. For example, if you prefer a dough without eggs or gluten, or if you want a heartier dough made with whole wheat flour, there's a recipe for that. The most traditional dough is made with just eggs and flour—no salt or oil is ever needed. And, although there are many more dough recipes, these recipes use common flours that are easy to find. There is also a four-in-one recipe, 4 Flavored Pasta Doughs (page 28), which offers four different flavorings for you to try.

TRADITIONAL EGG PASTA DOUGH

MAKES 1 POUND, ENOUGH TO SERVE 4

PREP TIME: 20 minutes | **REST TIME:** 30 minutes

DAIRY-FREE, NUT-FREE, VEGETARIAN

THIS RECIPE CREATES the classic egg pasta dough used in most stuffed pasta recipes. The eggs and Tipo "00" (a.k.a. double-zero) flour make the dough soft, smooth, elastic, and easy to work with.

2 cups (300 grams) Tipo "00" flour (or all-purpose flour), plus more for dusting

3 large eggs, at room temperature

1 large egg yolk, at room temperature

Water, as needed (see tip)

To make the dough by hand

1. Weigh or measure the flour onto a wooden pasta board or large cutting board. Make a wide, shallow well in the center of the flour and place the eggs and yolk in the well. Using a fork, beat the eggs in the center of the well until the yolks and whites are thoroughly blended.

2. Using the fork, scrape some of the flour from the inside edges of the flour well into the egg mixture and beat until the flour is absorbed into the egg. Repeat this step, gradually adding flour and beating until the egg mixture is no longer runny and begins to look shaggy.

3. Using a bench scraper, fold the mixture by sliding the scraper under the shaggy pile and turning it over multiple times until the dough comes together into a solid lump. Using your hands, gather the dough into a ball and set it aside. Use the bench scraper to scrape the pasta board clean of dried dough and discard the bits.

4. Knead the dough for 8 to 10 minutes, until the dough bounces back when pressed lightly with your finger.

5. Wrap the finished dough in plastic wrap and let it rest at room temperature for 30 minutes before rolling it out.

To make the dough using a food processor

1. In a 14-cup food processor fitted with the chopping blade, pulse the flour a few times to aerate it.

2. Crack the eggs and yolk into a small bowl. Turn on the food processor, and slowly pour the eggs through the feed tube. Process until a dough ball forms, then let the processor run for 2 to 3 minutes after the dough ball is formed. The inside of the bowl should be clean as the dough ball rotates around the blade. Do not leave the food processor unattended; it will move around while the dough ball spins around the bowl and may fall off the counter.

3. Wrap the finished dough in plastic wrap, and let it rest at room temperature for 30 minutes before rolling it out.

To make the dough using a stand mixer

1. In the bowl of a stand mixer fitted with the flat beater attachment, combine the flour, eggs, and egg yolk. Mix on speed 2 until the eggs are broken up and the flour is incorporated into their liquid.

2. Remove the beater attachment and replace it with the dough hook, scraping off any dough from the beater into the bowl. Mix on speed 2 for 5 minutes, until a dough ball forms and the dough bounces back when pressed lightly with your finger.

3. Wrap the finished dough in plastic wrap, and let it rest at room temperature for 30 minutes before rolling it out.

Ingredient tip: If the dough is sticking to your hands or to the sides of the processor/ bowl, add 1 tablespoon of flour at a time and mix it in. If the dough is crumbly and won't form into a ball, add 1 tablespoon of water at a time and mix it in until the dough is soft and pliable.

EGGLESS PASTA DOUGH

MAKES 1 POUND, ENOUGH TO SERVE 4

PREP TIME: 20 minutes | REST TIME: 30 minutes

DAIRY-FREE, NUT-FREE, VEGAN

EGGS ARE NOT required for pasta dough—flour and water work just as well if you prefer a vegan dough or just prefer not to use eggs.

2 cups (300 grams) Tipo "00" flour or all-purpose flour, plus more for dusting

½ cup (120 ml) warm water

To make the dough by hand

1. Weigh or measure the flour onto a wooden pasta board or large cutting board. Make a wide, shallow well in the center of the flour. Pour about half of the warm water into the center of the well.

2. Using a fork, scrape some of the flour from the inside edges of the well into the water and stir it in to make a slurry. Repeat this step, adding the remaining warm water a couple of tablespoons at a time, and gradually adding more flour to the water, mixing until the dough begins to look shaggy.

3. Using a bench scraper, fold the mixture by sliding the scraper under the shaggy pile and turning it over multiple times until the dough comes together into a solid lump. Using your hands, gather the dough into a ball and set it aside. Use the bench scraper to scrape the pasta board clean of dried dough and discard the bits.

4. Knead the dough for 8 to 10 minutes, until the dough bounces back when pressed lightly with your finger.

5. Wrap the finished dough in plastic wrap, and let it rest at room temperature for 30 minutes before rolling it out.

To make the dough using a food processor

1. In a 14-cup food processor fitted with the chopping blade, pulse the flour a few times to aerate it.

2. Turn on the food processor and slowly pour the water through the feed tube. Process until a dough ball forms, then let the processor run for 2 to 3 minutes after the dough ball is formed. The inside of the bowl should be clean as the dough ball rotates around the blade. Do not leave the food processor unattended; it will move around while the dough ball spins around the bowl.

3. Wrap the finished dough in plastic wrap, and let it rest at room temperature for 30 minutes before rolling it out.

To make the dough using a stand mixer

1. In the bowl of a stand mixer fitted with the flat beater attachment, combine the flour and water. Mix on speed 2 until the flour is incorporated into the liquid.

2. Remove the beater attachment and replace it with the dough hook, scraping off any dough from the beater into the bowl. Mix on speed 2 for 5 minutes, until a dough ball forms and the dough bounces back when pressed lightly with your finger.

3. Wrap the finished dough in plastic wrap, and let it rest at room temperature for 30 minutes before rolling it out.

Ingredient tip: Excluding the eggs here, which add protein to dough and help develop the gluten, means you may have to knead this dough for an extra minute or two to help the gluten form.

WHOLE WHEAT PASTA DOUGH

MAKES 1 POUND, ENOUGH TO SERVE 4

PREP TIME: 20 minutes | REST TIME: 30 minutes

DAIRY-FREE, NUT-FREE, VEGETARIAN

I PREFER TO use a 50:50 blend of whole wheat flour and Tipo "00" flour or all-purpose flour when making a wheat dough. Using 100 percent whole wheat flour results in a tougher dough that is sometimes difficult to work with, especially when making stuffed pasta, for which you need a pliable dough that will seal. If you want to use all whole wheat flour, use four large eggs, because the wheat flour absorbs more liquid.

1 cup (150 grams) whole wheat flour

1 cup (150 grams) Tipo "00" flour or all-purpose flour, plus more for dusting

3 large eggs, at room temperature

1 large egg yolk, at room temperature

To make the dough by hand

1. Weigh or measure the whole wheat flour and Tipo "00" flour into a large bowl and stir to blend. Pour the flour onto a wooden pasta board or large cutting board. Make a wide, shallow well in the center of the flour and place the eggs and egg yolk in the well. Using a fork, beat the eggs in the center of the well until the yolks and whites are thoroughly blended.

2. Using the fork, scrape some of the flour from the inside edges of the flour well into the egg mixture and beat until the flour is absorbed into the egg. Repeat this step, gradually adding flour and beating until the egg mixture is no longer runny and begins to look shaggy.

3. Using a bench scraper, fold the mixture by sliding the scraper under the shaggy pile and turning it over multiple times until the dough comes together into a solid lump. Using your hands, gather all the dough into a ball and set it aside. Use the bench scraper to scrape the pasta board clean of dried dough and discard the bits.

4. Knead the dough for 8 to 10 minutes, until the dough bounces back when pressed lightly with your finger.

5. Wrap the finished dough in plastic wrap, and let it rest at room temperature for 30 minutes before rolling it out.

To make the dough using a food processor

1. In a 14-cup food processor fitted with the chopping blade, combine both flours and pulse a few times to aerate and blend the flours.

2. Crack the eggs and yolk into a small bowl. Turn on the food processor, and slowly pour the eggs through the feed tube. Process until a dough ball forms, then let the processor run for 2 to 3 minutes after the dough ball is formed. The inside of the bowl should be clean as the dough ball rotates around the blade. Do not leave the food processor unattended; it will move around while the dough ball spins around the bowl.

3. Wrap the finished dough in plastic wrap, and let it rest at room temperature for 30 minutes before rolling it out.

To make the dough using a stand mixer

1. In the bowl of a stand mixer fitted with the flat beater attachment, combine both flours, the eggs, and egg yolk. Mix on speed 2 until the eggs are broken up and the flour is incorporated into their liquid.

2. Remove the beater attachment and replace it with the dough hook, scraping off any dough from the beater into the bowl. Mix on speed 2 for 5 minutes, until a dough ball forms and the dough bounces back when pressed lightly with your finger.

3. Wrap the finished dough in plastic wrap, and let it rest at room temperature for 30 minutes before rolling it out.

GLUTEN-FREE PASTA DOUGH

MAKES 1 POUND, ENOUGH TO SERVE 4

PREP TIME: 20 minutes

DAIRY-FREE, GLUTEN-FREE, NUT-FREE, VEGETARIAN

PROTEIN MAKES DOUGH elastic and pliable. When that protein is eliminated by using a gluten-free flour, it needs to be replaced with a stabilizer that mimics the characteristic of protein to act as a binder. Adding xanthan gum is one solution. Some gluten-free flour blends on the market already include this binder. Cup4Cup and King Arthur's Measure for Measure are two such blends that can be used as 1:1 substitutes for wheat flour. Note, because this dough contains no gluten, it does not need to rest before rolling it out.

2 cups (300 grams) Cup4Cup or Measure for Measure gluten-free flour blend, plus more for dusting	3 large eggs, at room temperature	1 large egg yolk, at room temperature

To make the dough by hand

1. Weigh or measure the flour blend onto a wooden pasta board or large cutting board. Make a wide, shallow well in the center of the flour blend and place the eggs and egg yolk in the well. Using a fork, beat the eggs in the center of the well until the yolks and whites are thoroughly blended.

2. Using the fork, scrape some of the flour blend from the inside edges of the flour well into the egg mixture and beat until the flour is absorbed into the egg. Repeat this step, gradually adding flour and beating until the egg mixture is incorporated into the flour.

3. Using a bench scraper, fold the mixture by sliding the scraper under the dough and turning it over multiple times until the dough comes together into a ball. Using your hands, gather the dough into a ball and set it aside. Use the bench scraper to scrape the pasta board clean of dried dough and discard the bits.

4. Knead the dough for 8 to 10 minutes, until the dough forms a ball that holds its shape and doesn't crumble. The dough will not be very elastic, but it should hold together when pressed lightly with your finger. Wrap the dough in plastic wrap until you're ready to use it.

Cooking tip: Because this is a tough dough, the food processor and stand mixer methods are not recommended for making it. This dough also won't be quite as pliable as other pasta doughs because it doesn't contain gluten. You will not be able to roll the dough quite as thin as dough made with gluten-containing flours, so roll the dough out slightly thicker—setting 4 on a pasta machine versus 5 or 6 for dough made with gluten-containing flour.

4 FLAVORED PASTA DOUGHS

MAKES 1 POUND, ENOUGH TO SERVE 4

PREP TIME: 20 minutes | **REST TIME:** 30 minutes

DAIRY-FREE, NUT-FREE, VEGAN OR VEGETARIAN

OPTIONS FOR CREATING colorful flavored pasta doughs are endless. Spinach is the most popular addition for this purpose, but you can use your favorite herbs, vegetables, spices, or even chocolate to flavor dough. I suggest some ideas here, but get creative and add different flavors or even try combinations of flavors such as basil with garlic and so on.

For green pasta dough

1 batch Traditional Egg Pasta Dough (page 20) or Eggless Pasta Dough (page 22), made with 1 cup minced fresh leafy greens (such as arugula, kale, or spinach) or fresh herbs (such as basil or parsley; if you wish to use dried herbs, see spiced or herbed dough, following)

For red pasta dough

1 batch Traditional Egg Pasta Dough (page 20) or Eggless Pasta Dough (page 22), made with ¼ cup pureed roasted beets, 1 (6-ounce) can tomato paste, or ¼ cup pureed roasted red peppers

For spiced or herbed pasta dough

1 batch Traditional Egg Pasta Dough (page 20) or Eggless Pasta Dough (page 22), made with

¼ cup dried spices or herbs (such as freshly ground black pepper, garlic powder, chili powder, lemon pepper seasoning, Italian seasoning, dried basil, or dried rosemary)

For chocolate pasta dough

1 batch Traditional Egg Pasta Dough (page 20) or Eggless Pasta Dough (page 22), made with ½ cup unsweetened cocoa powder

To make the dough by hand

1. Weigh or measure the flour onto a wooden pasta board or large cutting board. Make a wide, shallow well in the center of the flour and place the eggs and yolk (or water, for vegan pasta) and flavor additions into the well. Using a fork, beat the eggs and flavorings, or water and flavorings, in the center of the well until thoroughly blended.

2. Using the fork, scrape some of the flour from the inside edges of the flour well into the flavoring mixture, beating until the flour is absorbed into the liquid. Repeat this step, gradually adding flour and beating until the mixture is no longer runny and begins to look shaggy.

3. Using a bench scraper, fold the mixture by sliding the scraper under the shaggy pile and turning it over multiple times until the dough comes together into a solid lump. Using your hands, gather the dough into a ball and set it aside. Use the bench scraper to scrape the pasta board clean of dried dough and discard the bits.

4. Knead the dough for 8 to 10 minutes, until the dough bounces back when pressed lightly with your finger.

5. Wrap the finished dough in plastic wrap, and let it rest at room temperature for 30 minutes before rolling it out.

To make the dough using a food processor

1. In a 14-cup food processor fitted with the chopping blade, combine the flour and any flavor additions. Pulse a few times to aerate the flour and incorporate the flavorings.

CONTINUED

2. Crack the eggs and yolk into a small bowl. Turn on the food processor, and slowly pour the eggs through the feed tube. Process until the dough forms a ball, then let the processor run for 2 to 3 minutes after the dough ball is formed. The inside of the bowl should be clean as the dough ball rotates around the blade. Do not leave the food processor unattended; it will move around while the dough ball spins around the bowl.

3. Wrap the finished dough in plastic wrap, and let it rest at room temperature for 30 minutes before rolling it out.

To make the dough using a stand mixer

1. In the bowl of a stand mixer fitted with the flat beater attachment, combine the flour, eggs, egg yolk, and any flavorings. Mix on speed 2 until the eggs are broken up and the flour is incorporated into their liquid.

2. Remove the beater attachment and replace it with the dough hook, scraping off any dough from the beater into the bowl. Mix on speed 2 for 5 minutes, until a dough ball forms and the dough bounces back when pressed lightly with your finger.

3. Wrap the finished dough in plastic wrap, and let it rest at room temperature for 30 minutes before rolling it out.

> **Ingredient tip:** When adding wet ingredients, such as fresh greens or vegetable purees, you will need to add more flour than normal to account for the extra liquid. Add 1 tablespoon of flour at a time until the dough is no longer sticky.

SUN-DRIED TOMATO AND BASIL QUADRUCCI · 66

CRAB MEZZELUNE IN LEMON CREAM SAUCE · 60

CHAPTER THREE

RAVIOLI AND STUFFED PASTAS

EACH OF THE 30 recipes in this chapter includes detailed filling ingredients, a dough recommendation, and instructions for preparing the filling and shaping the dough, and finishes with a simple sauce or sauce recommendation from chapter 4. Feel free to experiment with any of these components—using a different dough or shape or filling or sauce. There is a mix-and-match chart with some ideas to get you started on page 113.

SPINACH AND ARTICHOKE RAVIOLI WITH CLASSIC MARINARA SAUCE

SERVES 6

PREP TIME: 1 hour 20 minutes | REST TIME: 30 minutes | COOK TIME: 25 minutes

NUT-FREE

SPINACH IS PROBABLY the most common and popular ingredient used in pasta fillings. Omit the artichoke to stick to tradition, if you prefer. I skip the laborious step of cooking the spinach and squeezing out the water—raw fresh spinach works great and saves time.

For the filling

2 cups whole milk ricotta cheese

2 cups marinated artichoke hearts, drained

1 cup tightly packed fresh spinach leaves

¼ cup grated Pecorino Romano cheese

⅛ teaspoon freshly grated or ground nutmeg

Salt

Freshly ground black pepper

For the pasta

Tipo "00" flour or all-purpose flour, for dusting

1 batch Traditional Egg Pasta Dough (page 20)

For serving

Salt

2 tablespoons salted butter

1 batch Classic Marinara Sauce (page 97), warmed

To make the filling

1. In a food processor, combine the ricotta, artichoke hearts, spinach, Pecorino Romano, and nutmeg and season with salt and pepper. Process until smooth. Scoop the filling into a piping bag or spoon it into a zip-top bag and cut off a bottom corner. Set aside.

To shape the pasta

1. Dust a baking sheet with flour.

2. Using a rolling pin or pasta machine roller, thin one-fourth of the dough into a sheet until you can just barely see your fingers through the pasta, as described on pages 12 to 14. Cut the sheet in half.

3. Rub flour on one side of one pasta sheet, then lay it on top of a ravioli mold, floured-side down. Use the press to make pockets in the sheet, then spoon or pipe about 1 tablespoon of filling into each of the pockets.

4. Lay the second pasta sheet on top and stretch it to cover the bottom sheet. Use a rolling pin to cut and seal the ravioli by rolling it over the mold in every direction. Remove the excess dough around the mold and flip the mold over to release the ravioli. Place the ravioli on the prepared baking sheet until you are ready to cook.

5. Repeat with the remaining dough and filling.

To cook and serve

1. Bring a large pot of salted water to a boil. Add the pasta and simmer for 4 to 5 minutes, until the ravioli float to the surface. Gently remove the ravioli with a skimmer or slotted spoon and shake out the excess water.

2. While the pasta cooks, in a large skillet or sauté pan over medium heat, melt the butter until it begins to foam.

3. Add the cooked ravioli to the melted butter and sauté for about 4 minutes on each side until crispy.

4. Serve the ravioli with the warmed marinara sauce on the side for dipping.

> **Cooking tip:** Do not forget to flour the bottom pasta sheet when using a ravioli mold, or the pasta will stick to the mold.

WHITE BEAN AND ROSEMARY TORTELLI WITH GREENS AND GARLIC

SERVES 4

PREP TIME: 1 hour 20 minutes | **REST TIME:** 30 minutes | **COOK TIME:** 15 minutes

DAIRY-FREE, NUT-FREE, VEGAN

TORTELLI IS YET another name for a stuffed pasta shape that is interchangeable with ravioli. In this recipe, we will stuff this creamy filling into standard 2-inch-square shapes. You can use a knife or stamp or ravioli mold to shape this filled pasta. Use a good, fruity extra-virgin olive oil for the filling. The topping for this pasta is garlicky spinach, but use any fresh greens you like.

For the filling

2 (15.5-ounce) cans cannellini beans, drained

½ cup extra-virgin olive oil

2 tablespoons fresh rosemary leaves, or 1½ teaspoons dried

2 tablespoons balsamic vinegar

Salt

Freshly ground black pepper

For the pasta

Tipo "00" flour or all-purpose flour, for dusting

1 batch Eggless Pasta Dough (page 22)

For serving

Salt

2 tablespoons extra-virgin olive oil, plus more for serving

1 garlic clove, minced

4 cups chopped fresh spinach leaves, kale, or chard

To make the filling

1. In a food processor, combine the beans, oil, rosemary, and vinegar and season with salt and pepper. Process until smooth. Scoop the filling into a pastry bag, or spoon it into a zip-top bag and cut off a bottom corner. Set aside.

To make the pasta

1. Dust a baking sheet with flour.

2. Using a rolling pin or pasta machine roller, thin one-fourth of the dough into a sheet until you can just barely see your fingers through the pasta, as described on pages 12 to 14. Cut the sheet in half.

3. Dust a clean work surface with flour and lay one of the half-sheets on it. Spoon or pipe the filling onto the sheet in 1-tablespoon dollops, spaced 2 inches apart on all sides (see page 14).

4. Lay the other half pasta sheet on top and gently press it down around the filling to seal and remove any air bubbles. Using a pastry cutter, stamp, or knife, cut the filled pockets into 2-inch squares. Place the tortelli on the prepared baking sheet until you are ready to cook.

5. Repeat with the remaining dough and filling.

To cook and serve

1. Bring a large pot of salted water to a boil. Add the pasta and simmer for 4 to 5 minutes, until the tortelli float to the surface. Gently remove the pasta with a skimmer or slotted spoon and shake out the excess water. Reserve 2 tablespoons of cooking water.

2. While the pasta cooks, in a large skillet or sauté pan over medium heat, combine the oil and garlic. Cook for 2 to 3 minutes, until the garlic is soft.

3. Add the greens and reserved pasta water and sauté for 3 to 4 minutes, until the liquid evaporates. Turn off the heat.

4. Add the cooked tortelli to the skillet and stir gently to coat with the sauce before serving.

Ingredient tip: Substitute 1 tablespoon grated lemon zest for the balsamic vinegar in the filling, or add it with the vinegar for some extra brightness.

FRESH RICOTTA RAVIOLINI IN WHITE BOLOGNESE SAUCE

SERVES 4

PREP TIME: 1 hour 20 minutes | **REST TIME:** 30 minutes | **COOK TIME:** 1 hour
COOL TIME: 20 minutes | **CHILL TIME:** 1 hour

NUT-FREE

THIS IS THE most basic ravioli filling—just cheese. But in this recipe, I show you a quick way to make your own fresh ricotta without all the fuss of adding an acid at the right time. Just combine milk and buttermilk and let science work its magic. Raviolini are small, square stuffed pasta.

For the filling

8 cups whole milk

2 cups buttermilk

Salt

½ cup grated Parmesan cheese

Dash freshly grated or ground nutmeg

Freshly ground black pepper

For the pasta

Tipo "00" flour or all-purpose flour, for dusting

1 batch Traditional Egg Pasta Dough (page 20)

For serving

Salt

1 batch White Bolognese (page 99)

¼ cup grated Parmesan cheese

To make the filling

1. In a large saucepan over medium heat, combine the milk and buttermilk. Cook for 30 to 40 minutes, until the mixture begins to simmer and curds start to form on top, stirring frequently to prevent scalding. Turn off the heat and let cool for 20 minutes.

2. Line a colander with cheesecloth, and use a ladle to slowly transfer the contents of the pot to the cheesecloth, trapping the curds and allowing the whey to drain. Refrigerate for about 1 hour to let the ricotta firm up. Add salt to taste.

3. In a large bowl, stir together the ricotta, ½ cup of Parmesan, nutmeg, and salt and pepper to taste until thoroughly combined. Set aside.

To make the pasta

1. Dust a baking sheet with flour.

2. Using a rolling pin or pasta machine roller, thin one-fourth of the dough into a sheet until you can just barely see your fingers through the pasta, as described on pages 12 to 14. Cut the sheet in half.

3. Dust a clean work surface with flour and lay one of the half-sheets on it. Spoon or pipe the filling onto the sheet in ½-tablespoon dollops, spaced 1 inch apart on all sides (see page 14).

4. Lay the other half pasta sheet on top and gently press it down around the filling to seal and remove any air bubbles. Using a pastry cutter, stamp, or knife, cut the filled pockets into 1-inch squares. Place the raviolini on the prepared baking sheet until you are ready to cook.

5. Repeat with the remaining dough and filling.

To cook and serve

1. Bring a large pot of salted water to a boil. Add the pasta and simmer for 4 to 5 minutes, until the raviolini float to the surface. Gently remove the pasta with a skimmer or slotted spoon and shake out the excess water. Reserve ¼ cup of pasta cooking water.

2. In a large skillet or sauté pan over medium heat, heat the Bolognese sauce for about 5 minutes, until warmed though.

3. Turn the heat to medium-high and stir in the reserved pasta water and Parmesan. Simmer for 1 minute to thin the sauce.

4. Add the raviolini, stir to coat with the sauce, and serve.

Cooking tip: Try the Sunday Sauce (page 103) if you prefer a red sauce to go with this pasta.

PUMPKIN TORTELLI WITH BUTTER, SAGE, AND PARMESAN

SERVES 4

PREP TIME: 1 hour 20 minutes | **REST TIME:** 30 minutes | **COOK TIME:** 40 minutes

NUT-FREE

THIS SQUARE PASTA is called *tortelli di zucca* in Italy. In Italian, *zucca* means "pumpkin." Italian pumpkins are smaller, sweeter, and less stringy than the large pumpkins found in the United States, so this recipe uses canned pumpkin, baked to reduce the moisture as well as to sweeten the flavor.

For the filling

2 (15-ounce) cans pumpkin puree

½ cup (2 ounces) amaretti cookies, crushed into crumbs

¼ cup grated Parmesan cheese

½ teaspoon ground cinnamon

⅛ teaspoon freshly grated or ground nutmeg

Salt

Freshly ground black pepper

For the pasta

Tipo "00" flour or all-purpose flour, for dusting

1 batch Traditional Egg Pasta Dough (page 20)

For serving

Salt

4 tablespoons (½ stick) salted butter

3 or 4 fresh sage leaves

Grated Parmesan cheese

To make the filling

1. Preheat the oven to 400°F. Line a baking sheet with parchment paper.

2. Spread the pumpkin thinly, less than ¼ inch thick, over the parchment.

3. Bake for 25 minutes, until the edges start to brown and most of the liquid is cooked off. Let cool for 10 minutes.

4. In a large bowl, combine the pumpkin, cookie crumbs, Parmesan, cinnamon, and nutmeg and season with salt and pepper. Stir until the ingredients are thoroughly combined.

To make the pasta

1. Dust a baking sheet with flour.

2. Using a rolling pin or pasta machine roller, thin one-fourth of the dough into a sheet until you can just barely see your fingers through the pasta, as described on pages 12 to 14. Cut the sheet in half.

3. Dust a clean work surface with flour and lay one of the half-sheets on it. Spoon or pipe the filling onto the sheet in 1-tablespoon dollops, spaced 2 inches apart on all sides (see page 14).

4. Lay the other half pasta sheet on top and gently press it down around the filling to seal and remove any air bubbles. Using a pastry cutter, stamp, or knife, cut the filled pockets into 2-inch squares. Place the tortelli on the prepared baking sheet until you are ready to cook.

5. Repeat with the remaining dough and filling.

To cook and serve

1. Bring a large pot of salted water to a boil. Add the pasta and simmer for 4 to 5 minutes, until the tortelli float to the surface. Gently remove the pasta with a skimmer or slotted spoon and shake out the excess water.

2. In a large skillet or sauté pan over medium heat, combine the butter and sage leaves. Cook for about 3 minutes, until the butter melts and starts to foam. Turn the heat to low and cook for 4 to 5 minutes, stirring frequently, until light-brown specks begin to form in the skillet.

3. Add the tortelli and stir to coat. Top with Parmesan before serving.

Ingredient tip: When using canned pumpkin, the only ingredient on the can's label should be pumpkin—do not use pumpkin pie filling.

EGGPLANT PARMESAN RAVIOLI IN CLASSIC MARINARA SAUCE

SERVES 4-6

PREP TIME: 1 hour 20 minutes | **REST TIME:** 30 minutes | **COOK TIME:** 35 minutes

NUT-FREE

THIS RAVIOLI IS a combination of everyone's favorite Italian classic dish, eggplant Parmesan, and elements of the tangy Sicilian eggplant condiment called caponata.

For the filling

2 tablespoons extra-virgin olive oil

3 garlic cloves, minced

1 cup diced onion

½ teaspoon red pepper flakes

5 cups diced eggplant (1 pound)

2 cups diced bell pepper, any color (2 medium)

1 (6-ounce) can tomato paste

1 tablespoon red wine vinegar

Salt

Freshly ground black pepper

¼ cup grated Parmesan cheese

½ cup shredded mozzarella cheese

For the pasta

Whole wheat or all-purpose flour, for dusting

1 batch Whole Wheat Pasta Dough (page 24)

For serving

Salt

1 batch Classic Marinara Sauce (page 97), warmed

To make the filling

1. In a large (4- to 5-quart) saucepan over medium heat, heat the oil. Add the garlic, onion, and red pepper flakes. Sauté for about 5 minutes, until the garlic and onion are soft. Reduce the heat to medium-low, add the eggplant and bell pepper, and cook for 10 minutes, stirring often.

2. Stir in the tomato paste, vinegar, and salt and pepper to taste, stirring until the tomato paste is thoroughly combined with the vegetables. Simmer for 10 minutes, then let cool.

3. Transfer the cooled filling to a food processor, add the Parmesan, and puree until smooth.

4. Remove the blade and stir in the mozzarella.

To make the pasta

1. Dust a baking sheet with flour.

2. Using a rolling pin or pasta machine roller, thin one-fourth of the dough into a sheet until you can just barely see your fingers through the pasta, as described on pages 12 to 14. Cut the sheet in half.

3. Dust a clean work surface with flour and lay one of the half-sheets on it. Spoon or pipe the filling onto the sheet in 1-tablespoon dollops, spaced 2 inches apart on all sides (see page 14).

4. Lay the other half pasta sheet on top and gently press it down around the filling to seal and remove any air bubbles. Using a pastry cutter, stamp, or knife, cut the filled pockets into squares. Place the ravioli on the prepared baking sheet until you are ready to cook.

5. Repeat with the remaining dough and filling.

To cook and serve

1. Bring a large pot of salted water to a boil. Add the pasta and simmer for 4 to 5 minutes, until the ravioli float to the surface. Gently remove the pasta with a skimmer or slotted spoon and shake out the excess water.

2. Serve the ravioli with the warmed marinara sauce.

Cooking tip: This recipe yields a large amount of caponata. You can serve the extra on toasted bread or freeze it for later use.

TUSCAN POTATO TORTELLI IN BEEF, RED BELL PEPPER, AND TOMATO SAUCE

SERVES 4

PREP TIME: 1 hour 20 minutes | **REST TIME:** 30 minutes | **COOK TIME:** 40 minutes

NUT-FREE

THE TRADITIONAL ITALIAN name for this pasta is *tortelli Mugello*. Mugello is a valley in the northern part of Tuscany. This tortelli recipe is a rustic and hearty stuffed pasta made with potato, cheese, and garlic, and tinged red with tomato paste. Tortelli Mugello is traditionally served with a meat sauce or sage and butter sauce.

For the filling

1 pound white or yellow starchy potatoes, peeled

Salt

2 tablespoons salted butter

2 garlic cloves, minced

2 tablespoons minced fresh parsley

1 (6-ounce) can tomato paste

2 tablespoons heavy (whipping) cream

½ cup grated Parmesan cheese, plus more for serving

Freshly ground black pepper

For the pasta

Whole wheat or all-purpose flour, for dusting

1 batch Whole Wheat Pasta Dough (page 24)

For serving

Salt

1 batch Beef, Red Bell Pepper, and Tomato Sauce (page 107), warmed

To make the filling

1. In a large pot, combine the potatoes with enough cold water to cover. Generously season the water with salt. Bring to a boil and cook the potatoes for about 15 minutes, until tender. Drain and let cool.

2. Meanwhile, in a small pan over medium heat, melt the butter with the garlic, then cook for 2 minutes, until fragrant. Add the parsley and cook for 2 minutes.

3. Using a wooden spoon, stir in the tomato paste, mashing to combine it with the garlic mixture. Cook for 5 minutes, stirring often, until lightly browned.

4. In a large bowl, combine the cooked, cooled potatoes and heavy cream. Using a potato masher, mash until smooth. Add the tomato paste mixture and the Parmesan and stir until combined. Season with salt and pepper to taste.

To make the pasta

1. Dust a baking sheet with flour.

2. Using a rolling pin or pasta machine roller, thin one-fourth of the dough into a sheet until you can just barely see your fingers through the pasta, as described on pages 12 to 14. Cut the sheet in half.

3. Dust a clean work surface with flour and lay one of the half-sheets on it. Spoon or pipe the filling onto the sheet in 1-tablespoon dollops, spaced 2 inches apart on all sides (see page 14).

4. Lay the other half pasta sheet on top and gently press it down around the filling to seal and remove any air bubbles. Using a pastry cutter, stamp, or knife, cut out the filled pockets. Place the tortelli on the prepared baking sheet until you are ready to cook.

5. Repeat with the remaining dough and filling.

To cook and serve

1. Bring a large pot of salted water to a boil. Add the pasta and simmer for 4 to 5 minutes, until the tortelli float to the surface. Gently remove the pasta with a skimmer or slotted spoon and shake out the excess water.

2. Serve the pasta with the warmed Beef, Red Bell Pepper, and Tomato Sauce.

Variation tip: To make this tortelli "Pratese," from another nearby Tuscan town, Prato, add 8 ounces cooked ground beef seasoned with salt and pepper, 1 large egg, and a pinch of freshly grated nutmeg to the mixing bowl in step 4.

SAUSAGE AND PEPPER MEZZELUNE WITH CLASSIC MARINARA SAUCE

SERVES 4

PREP TIME: 1 hour 20 minutes | **REST TIME:** 30 minutes | **COOK TIME:** 30 minutes

NUT-FREE

THIS RECIPE IS based on a favorite Italian American festival and party food—grilled sausage with peppers and onions. If you like things spicy, substitute hot Italian sausage. *Mezzelune* means "half-moon" in Italian, so this filled pasta is a semicircular shape.

For the filling

1 tablespoon extra-virgin olive oil

8 ounces sweet Italian sausage, casings removed

1 medium red bell pepper, chopped

¼ cup chopped onion

1 cup whole milk ricotta cheese

½ cup shredded provolone cheese

Salt

Freshly ground black pepper

For the pasta

Tipo "00" flour or all-purpose flour, for dusting

1 batch Eggless Pasta Dough (page 22)

For serving

Salt

1 batch Classic Marinara Sauce (page 97), warmed

To make the filling

1. In a large skillet or sauté pan over medium heat, heat the oil for 1 minute. Add the sausage and cook for 8 to 10 minutes, until browned. Remove the sausage and set it aside, then add the bell pepper and onion to the skillet. Sauté for 6 to 8 minutes, until the pepper and onion are soft and just starting to brown. Remove from the heat and let cool.

2. Transfer the cooled sausage, bell pepper, and onion to a large mixing bowl. Add the ricotta and provolone and season with salt and pepper. Stir until well combined.

To make the pasta

1. Dust a baking sheet with flour.

2. Using a rolling pin or pasta machine roller, thin one-fourth of the dough into a sheet until you can just barely see your fingers through the pasta, as described on pages 12 to 14.

3. Dust a clean work surface with flour and lay the pasta sheet on it. Using a ravioli stamp, cookie cutter, or large drinking glass, cut 3-inch circles from the dough.

4. Place 1 rounded tablespoon of filling ¼ inch from the edge of each circle. Fold the circles in half over the filling, making a half-moon shape. Use your fingers to seal the edges securely. Place the pasta on the prepared baking sheet until you are ready to cook.

5. Repeat with the remaining dough and filling.

To cook and serve

1. Bring a large pot of salted water to a boil. Add the pasta and simmer for 4 to 5 minutes, until the mezzelune float to the surface. Gently remove the pasta with a skimmer or slotted spoon and shake out the excess water.

2. Serve the pasta with the warmed marinara sauce.

"UTICA GREENS" RAVIOLI

SERVES 4

PREP TIME: 1 hour 20 minutes | **REST TIME:** 30 minutes | **COOK TIME:** 25 minutes

NUT-FREE

THIS GARLICKY, CHEESY concoction uses a favorite Italian ingredient, escarole—a slightly bitter green. Utica greens are a popular dish around the Italian American areas of Central New York. There are many different recipes for it, but most include escarole, lots of garlic, and hot cherry peppers. My recipe turns this regional favorite into a stuffed pasta filling.

For the filling

2 tablespoons salted butter

½ cup diced prosciutto

½ cup chopped onion

3 garlic cloves, minced

1 head escarole, rinsed and chopped

¼ cup water

¼ cup diced pickled hot cherry peppers

Salt

Freshly ground black pepper

1 cup whole milk ricotta

½ cup grated Pecorino Romano cheese, plus more for serving

¼ cup shredded sharp provolone cheese

¼ cup panko bread crumbs

For the pasta

Whole wheat or all-purpose flour, for dusting

1 batch Whole Wheat Pasta Dough (page 24)

For serving

Salt

2 tablespoons extra-virgin olive oil

Grated Pecorino Romano cheese

To make the filling

1. In a large skillet or sauté pan over medium heat, melt the butter. Add the prosciutto, onion, and garlic and cook for 4 to 5 minutes, until the prosciutto starts to brown.

2. Add the escarole, water, and cherry peppers to the skillet. Season with salt and pepper to taste. Cook for about 5 minutes, stirring, until the escarole wilts and the water cooks off. Let cool.

3. In a large food processor, combine the escarole mixture, ricotta, Pecorino Romano, provolone, and panko bread crumbs. Process until combined but not fully pureed. Taste and season with salt and pepper, if needed.

To make the pasta

1. Dust a baking sheet with flour.

2. Using a rolling pin or pasta machine roller, thin one-fourth of the dough into a sheet until you can just barely see your fingers through the pasta, as described on pages 12 to 14.

3. Dust a clean work surface with flour and lay the pasta sheet on it. Use a knife to cut the pasta into 3-by-2-inch rectangles.

4. Spoon 1 tablespoon of filling onto the bottom third of the rectangles. Fold the top half of the rectangles over the filling. Use the tines of a fork to seal the edges securely on the three open sides. Place the pasta on the prepared baking sheet until you are ready to cook.

5. Repeat with the remaining dough and filling.

To cook and serve

1. Bring a large pot of salted water to a boil. Add the pasta and simmer for 4 to 5 minutes, until it floats to the surface. Gently remove the pasta with a skimmer or slotted spoon and shake out the excess water

2. Drizzle with olive oil and top with Pecorino Romano.

Ingredient tip: If you cannot find escarole, use kale or Swiss chard, tough center ribs removed, as a substitute.

PIZZOCCHERI-STYLE WHOLE WHEAT RAVIOLI IN SAGE BUTTER SAUCE

SERVES 4

PREP TIME: 1 hour 20 minutes | **REST TIME:** 30 minutes | **COOK TIME:** 35 minutes

NUT-FREE

THIS FILLING IS based on *pizzoccheri*—the buttery baked pasta that people eat after a day of skiing in the Italian Alps in Lombardy. I used the elements from this casserole-style dish to make a hearty filling. Whole Wheat Pasta Dough is a good substitute for the buckwheat pasta that is traditionally used for this dish.

For the filling

1 pound potatoes, peeled

Salt

4 tablespoons (½ stick) salted butter

1 cup diced speck, smoked ham, or cooked bacon

2 garlic cloves, minced

2 fresh sage leaves

1 pound cabbage, finely chopped

1 cup shredded fontina cheese

¼ cup grated Parmesan cheese, plus more for serving

Freshly ground black pepper

For the pasta

Whole wheat or all-purpose flour, for dusting

1 batch Whole Wheat Pasta Dough (page 24)

For serving

Salt

4 tablespoons (½ stick) salted butter

2 fresh sage leaves

To make the filling

1. In a large pot, combine the potatoes with enough cold water to cover. Generously season the water with salt. Bring to a boil over medium heat and cook the potatoes for about 15 minutes, until tender. Drain and let cool.

2. Meanwhile, in a large skillet or sauté pan over medium heat, melt the butter. Add the speck and cook for 3 to 4 minutes, until it begins to brown. Add the garlic and sage leaves and cook for 3 minutes. Remove and discard the sage.

3. Adjust the heat to medium-low, add the cabbage to the pan, and stir to coat with the butter mixture. Cook for 8 to 10 minutes, stirring often, until the cabbage is softened. Remove from heat and let cool.

4. In a large bowl, mash the potatoes until smooth. Add the cabbage mixture, fontina, and Parmesan and season with salt and pepper.

To make the pasta

1. Dust a baking sheet with flour.

2. Using a rolling pin or pasta machine roller, thin one-fourth of the dough into a sheet until you can just barely see your fingers through the pasta, as described on pages 12 to 14. Cut the sheet in half.

3. Dust a clean work surface with flour and lay one of the half-sheets on it. Spoon or pipe the filling onto the sheet in 1-tablespoon dollops, spaced 2 inches apart on all sides (see page 14).

4. Lay the other half pasta sheet on top and gently press it down around the filling to seal and remove any air bubbles. Using a pastry cutter, stamp, or knife, cut the filled pockets into squares. Place the ravioli on the prepared baking sheet until you are ready to cook.

5. Repeat with the remaining dough and filling.

To cook and serve

1. Bring a large pot of salted water to a boil. Add the pasta and simmer for 4 to 5 minutes, until the ravioli float to the surface. Gently remove the pasta with a skimmer or slotted spoon and shake out the excess water

2. In a large skillet or sauté pan over medium heat, melt the butter. Add the sage leaves and cook for 2 to 3 minutes, until the butter is foaming. Add the pasta to the pan and gently stir to coat with sauce.

'NDUJA AND BURRATA TRIANGLES WITH NO-COOK TOMATO AND CASTELVETRANO OLIVE SAUCE

SERVES 4

PREP TIME: 1 hour 20 minutes | **REST TIME:** 30 minutes | **COOK TIME:** 10 minutes

NUT-FREE

'NDUJA AND BURRATA cheese are traditional ingredients of Southern Italian cooking that have recently been discovered by cooks around the world. 'Nduja, from Calabria on the toe of Italy, is a spicy spreadable salami. Burrata, from Puglia on the heel of Italy, is a ball of fresh mozzarella with curds and cream inside.

For the filling

2 cups whole milk ricotta

1 cup 'nduja

1 cup burrata

Salt

Freshly ground black pepper

For the pasta

Tipo "00" flour or all-purpose flour, for dusting

1 batch Eggless Pasta Dough (page 22)

For serving

Salt

1 batch No-Cook Tomato and Castelvetrano Olive Sauce (page 104)

To make the filling

1. In a large food processor, combine the ricotta and 'nduja. Process until thoroughly combined.

2. In a large bowl, chop the burrata into small pieces. Be sure to do this in a bowl to contain the soft creamy filling inside the burrata, so you can stir it in with the chopped pieces. Add the ricotta and 'nduja mixture to the chopped burrata and stir until thoroughly combined. Season with salt and pepper.

To make the pasta

1. Dust a baking sheet with flour.

2. Using a rolling pin or pasta machine roller, thin one-fourth of the dough into a sheet until you can just barely see your fingers through the pasta, as described on pages 12 to 14.

3. Dust a clean work surface with flour and lay the pasta sheet on it. Use a knife to cut the pasta into 3-inch squares.

4. Place 1 rounded tablespoon of filling near one corner of each square. Fold the top half of the squares over the filling to form triangles. Use your fingers to seal the edges securely. Trim the edges with a knife or fluted pastry cutter. Place the pasta on the prepared baking sheet until you are ready to cook.

5. Repeat with the remaining dough and filling.

To cook and serve

1. Bring a large pot of salted water to a boil. Add the pasta and simmer for 4 to 5 minutes, until the triangles float to the surface. Gently remove the pasta with a skimmer or slotted spoon and shake out the excess water.

2. Serve the pasta with the No-Cook Tomato and Castelvetrano Olive Sauce.

PESTO PANSOTTI IN MUSHROOM RAGÙ

SERVES 4

PREP TIME: 1 hour 20 minutes | **REST TIME:** 30 minutes | **COOK TIME:** 10 minutes

THIS DISH CELEBRATES the food of Genoa in Liguria. *Pansotti*, which means "little bellies" in the Genovese dialect, is a traditional shape from the region. It is a pasta triangle filled with a generous amount of stuffing to resemble a pot belly. Basil pesto also hails from Genoa, so this is a good pairing.

For the filling

2 cups tightly packed fresh basil leaves

½ cup grated Parmesan cheese

¼ cup pine nuts

1 garlic clove, peeled

Salt

Freshly ground black pepper

¼ cup extra-virgin olive oil

1 cup whole milk ricotta cheese

For the pasta

Whole wheat or all-purpose flour, for dusting

1 batch Whole Wheat Pasta Dough (page 24)

For serving

Salt

1 batch Mushroom Ragù (page 102), warmed

To make the filling

1. In a food processor, combine the basil, Parmesan, pine nuts, and garlic and season with salt and pepper. Turn on the processor and slowly drizzle in the oil. Blend for 2 to 3 minutes, until smooth, stopping once to scrape down the sides about halfway through.

2. Add the ricotta and blend until combined.

To make the pasta

1. Dust a baking sheet with flour.

2. Using a rolling pin or pasta machine roller, thin one-fourth of the dough into a sheet until you can just barely see your fingers through the pasta, as described on pages 12 to 14. Cut the sheet in half.

3. Dust a clean work surface with flour and lay one of the half-sheets on it. Spoon or pipe the filling onto the sheet in 1-tablespoon dollops, spaced 2 inches apart on all sides (see page 14).

4. Lay the other half pasta sheet on top and gently press it down around the filling to seal and remove any air bubbles. Using a fluted pastry cutter or knife, cut diagonally between the filled pockets to create regular triangular shapes. Place the pansotti on the prepared baking sheet until you are ready to cook.

5. Repeat with the remaining dough and filling.

To cook and serve

1. Bring a large pot of salted water to a boil. Add the pasta and simmer for 4 to 5 minutes, until the pansotti float to the surface. Gently remove the pasta with a skimmer or slotted spoon and shake out the excess water.

2. Serve the pasta with the warmed Mushroom Ragù.

ROASTED CAULIFLOWER RAVIOLONE IN PESTO CREAM SAUCE

SERVES 4

PREP TIME: 1 hour 20 minutes | **REST TIME:** 30 minutes | **COOK TIME:** 40 minutes

GLUTEN-FREE

THE ITALIAN LANGUAGE adds a suffix to a word to define size. Anything ending in "-one" means large. A raviolone, then, is a large ravioli. Anything ending with "ini" means little, such as raviolini.

For the filling

1 large (2-pound) head cauliflower, trimmed and cut into large florets

1 tablespoon extra-virgin olive oil

Salt

Freshly ground black pepper

½ cup whole milk ricotta

½ cup grated Parmesan cheese

½ cup (4 ounces) mascarpone cheese

2 tablespoons heavy (whipping) cream (optional)

For the pasta

Gluten-free flour, for dusting

1 batch Gluten-Free Pasta Dough (page 26)

For serving

Salt

1 batch Pesto Cream Sauce (page 101)

To make the filling

1. Preheat the oven to 400°F.

2. In a large bowl, combine the cauliflower and oil and season with salt and pepper. Stir to coat the florets. Transfer the cauliflower to a baking sheet lined with parchment paper or aluminum foil and spread it into an even layer.

3. Bake for 25 to 30 minutes, stirring once halfway through, until the cauliflower begins to caramelize. Let cool for 10 minutes.

4. In a food processor, combine the cooled cauliflower, ricotta, Parmesan, and mascarpone. Process until smooth. Add the heavy cream, if needed, to thin out the filling. Taste and season with salt and pepper.

To make the pasta

1. Dust a baking sheet with flour.

2. Using a rolling pin or pasta machine roller, thin one-fourth of the dough into a sheet until you can just barely see your fingers through the pasta, as described on pages 12 to 14. Cut the sheet in half.

3. Dust a clean work surface with flour and lay one of the half-sheets on it. Spoon or pipe the filling onto the sheet in 2-tablespoon dollops, spaced 3 inches apart on all sides (see page 14).

4. Lay the other half pasta sheet on top and gently press it down around the filling to seal and remove any air bubbles. Using a fluted pastry cutter or a knife, cut the filled pockets into 3-inch squares. Place the raviolone on the prepared baking sheet until you are ready to cook.

5. Repeat with the remaining dough and filling.

To cook and serve

1. Bring a large pot of salted water to a boil. Add the pasta, 3 to 4 at a time, and simmer for 4 to 5 minutes, until the raviolone float to the surface. Gently remove the pasta with a skimmer or slotted spoon and shake out the excess water. Repeat with the remaining pasta.

2. Serve the pasta with the Pesto Cream Sauce.

SHORT RIB LUNE

SERVES 4

PREP TIME: 1 hour 20 minutes | **REST TIME:** 30 minutes | **COOK TIME:** 3 hours 30 minutes

NUT-FREE

LUNE **MEANS "MOON"** in Italian. This large, circle-shaped pasta is full of meat from short ribs that have been braised in a rich tomato base until the meat just falls off the bone. Use the sauce made from cooking the ribs to top the pasta.

For the filling

2½ pounds short ribs

Salt

Freshly ground black pepper

2 tablespoons extra-virgin olive oil

½ cup minced onion

½ cup minced carrot

½ cup minced celery

2 garlic cloves, minced

2 cups beef broth

2 (6-ounce) cans tomato paste

1 tablespoon minced fresh rosemary leaves, or 1 teaspoon dried

2 tablespoons panko bread crumbs

2 tablespoons milk

2 large eggs

¼ cup grated Parmesan cheese

For the pasta

Whole wheat or all-purpose flour, for dusting

1 batch Whole Wheat Pasta Dough (page 24)

To make the filling

1. Preheat the oven to 325°F.

2. Season the short ribs on all sides with salt and pepper. In a Dutch oven over medium heat, heat the oil. Add the ribs to the pot and cook for about 10 minutes, turning, until the ribs are browned on all sides. Transfer the ribs to a bowl.

3. Add the onion, carrot, celery, and garlic to the pot and cook for 6 to 8 minutes, until soft and golden.

4. Stir in the broth, tomato paste, and rosemary and bring to a simmer. Return the short ribs to the pot along with any juices from the bowl. Cover the pot with a lid and transfer it to the oven.

5. Braise for 2 to 2½ hours, until the ribs are tender. Transfer the ribs to a cutting board or plate and let them cool. Shred the meat and discard the bones.

6. In a small bowl, stir together the panko bread crumbs and milk; set aside for 5 minutes so the bread can absorb the liquid.

7. In a large bowl, combine the short rib meat, eggs, soaked panko bread crumbs, and Parmesan. Season to taste with salt and pepper.

To make the pasta

1. Dust a baking sheet with flour.

2. Using a rolling pin or pasta machine roller, thin one-fourth of the dough into a sheet until you can just barely see your fingers through the pasta, as described on pages 12 to 14. Cut the sheet in half.

3. Dust a clean work surface with flour and lay one of the half-sheets on it. Spoon or pipe the filling onto the sheet in 1-tablespoon dollops, spaced 2 inches apart on all sides (see page 14).

4. Lay the other half pasta sheet on top and gently press it down around the filling to seal and remove any air bubbles. Using a 2-inch round ravioli stamp or drinking glass, press to cut and seal the pasta around the filling. Place the lune on the prepared baking sheet until you are ready to cook.

5. Repeat with the remaining dough and filling.

To cook and serve

1. Bring a large pot of salted water to a boil. Add the pasta and simmer for 4 to 5 minutes, until the lune float to the surface. Gently remove the pasta with a skimmer or slotted spoon and shake out the excess water.

2. Meanwhile, on the stovetop over medium heat, reheat the braising liquid for about 5 minutes until warmed though.

3. Turn off the heat. Add the lune to the pot and stir to coat.

CRAB MEZZELUNE IN LEMON CREAM SAUCE

SERVES 4

PREP TIME: 1 hour 20 minutes | **REST TIME:** 30 minutes | **COOK TIME:** 10 minutes

NUT-FREE

THIS IS A great addition to a seafood-centered menu such as the traditional Feast of the Seven Fishes on Christmas Eve. It is sometimes hard to find seven different fish dishes, so why not add a stuffed crab pasta to the menu?

For the filling

2 (6-ounce) cans lump crabmeat

8 ounces cream cheese, at room temperature

1 cup whole milk ricotta

1 shallot, minced

2 tablespoons minced fresh parsley, or 1 tablespoon dried

Grated zest of 1 lemon

Salt

Freshly ground black pepper

For the pasta

Whole wheat or all-purpose flour, for dusting

1 batch Whole Wheat Pasta Dough (page 24)

For serving

Salt

1 batch Lemon Cream Sauce (page 105), gently warmed

To make the filling

1. In a large bowl, stir together the crab, cream cheese, ricotta, shallot, parsley, and lemon zest. Season with salt and pepper and stir until thoroughly combined.

To make the pasta

1. Dust a baking sheet with flour.

2. Using a rolling pin or pasta machine roller, thin one-fourth of the dough into a sheet until you can just barely see your fingers through the pasta, as described on pages 12 to 14.

3. Dust a clean work surface with flour and lay the pasta sheet on it. Use a 3-inch round ravioli stamp, cookie cutter, or large drinking glass to cut the pasta into circles.

4. Place 1 rounded tablespoon of filling ¼ inch from the edge of each circle. Fold the circles in half, making half-moon shapes. Use your fingers to seal the edges securely. Place the pasta on the prepared baking sheet until you are ready to cook.

5. Repeat with the remaining dough and filling.

To cook and serve

1. Bring a large pot of salted water to a boil. Add the pasta and simmer for 4 to 5 minutes, until the mezzelune float to the surface. Gently remove the pasta with a skimmer or slotted spoon and shake out the excess water.

2. Serve the pasta with the warmed Lemon Cream Sauce.

PUREED PEA AND MINT TRIANGLES WITH ROASTED TOMATO AND THYME SAUCE

SERVES 4

PREP TIME: 1 hour 20 minutes | **REST TIME:** 30 minutes | **COOK TIME:** 10 minutes

DAIRY-FREE, NUT-FREE, VEGAN

YOU CAN MAKE any pasta filling vegan, as long as the ingredients have enough body to be spooned or piped onto the dough. Pureed peas make a great filling without any cheese, though you can always add ½ cup or so of ricotta if you prefer a creamier filling.

For the filling

2 tablespoons extra-virgin olive oil

¼ cup chopped shallot

1 pound frozen peas, thawed

Salt

Freshly ground black pepper

½ cup tightly packed fresh mint leaves

For the pasta

Tipo "00" flour or all-purpose flour, for dusting

1 batch Eggless Pasta Dough (page 22)

For serving

Salt

1 batch Roasted Tomato and Thyme Sauce (page 98), warmed

To make the filling

1. In a large skillet or sauté pan over medium heat, combine the oil and shallot. Cook for 2 minutes, stirring occasionally, until the shallot is softened. Add the peas and season with salt and pepper. Cook for 4 minutes, until warmed through. Transfer the pea mixture to a food processor and add the mint. Process until smooth, stopping once to scrape down the sides of the bowl about halfway through.

To make the pasta

1. Dust a baking sheet with flour.

2. Using a rolling pin or pasta machine roller, thin one-fourth of the dough into a sheet until you can just barely see your fingers through the pasta, as described on pages 12 to 14.

3. Dust a clean work surface with flour and lay the pasta sheet on it. Use a knife to cut the pasta into 3-inch squares.

4. Place 1 rounded tablespoon of filling near one corner of each square. Fold the top half of the squares over the filling to form triangles. Use your fingers to seal the edges securely. Trim the edges with a knife or fluted pastry cutter. Place the pasta on the prepared baking sheet until you are ready to cook.

5. Repeat with the remaining dough and filling.

To cook and serve

1. Bring a large pot of salted water to a boil. Add the pasta and simmer for 4 to 5 minutes, until the triangles float to the surface. Gently remove the pasta with a skimmer or slotted spoon and shake out the excess water.

2. Serve the pasta with the warmed Roasted Tomato and Thyme Sauce.

Variation tip: Substitute basil in an equal amount and the grated zest of one lemon for the mint, or try a combination of flavors to add a twist to the filling.

OLIVE AND PROVOLONE FRANCOBOLLI WITH ARUGULA AND ALMOND PESTO

SERVES 4

PREP TIME: 1 hour 20 minutes | **REST TIME:** 30 minutes | **COOK TIME:** 10 minutes

THE FILLING HAS a strong olive flavor, so a smaller pasta shape works best for it. Luckily, the Italians have a shape just for this filling called *francobolli*, which translates to "postage stamp." You may not need to add salt to this filling because the olives are salty, so taste it first before adding.

For the filling

2 cups whole milk ricotta

1 cup mixed pitted olives

½ cup shredded sharp provolone cheese

Salt

Freshly ground black pepper

For the pasta

Tipo "00" flour or all-purpose flour, for dusting

1 batch Eggless Pasta Dough (page 22)

For serving

Salt

1 batch Arugula and Almond Pesto (page 109)

To make the filling

1. In a food processor, combine the ricotta and olives. Process until smooth, stopping once to scrape down the sides of the bowl about halfway through.

2. Remove the blade and stir in the provolone until thoroughly combined. Taste and season with salt and pepper.

To make the pasta

1. Dust a baking sheet with flour.

2. Using a rolling pin or pasta machine roller, thin one-fourth of the dough into a sheet until you can just barely see your fingers through the pasta as described on pages 12 to 14. Cut the sheet in half.

3. Dust a clean work surface with flour and lay one of the half-sheets on it. Spoon or pipe the filling onto the sheet in ¼-teaspoon dollops, spaced 1 inch apart on all sides (see page 14).

4. Lay the other half pasta sheet on top and gently press it down around the filling to seal and remove any air bubbles. Using a pastry cutter, stamp, or knife, cut the filled pockets into 1-inch squares. Place the francobolli on the prepared baking sheet until you are ready to cook.

5. Repeat with the remaining dough and filling.

To cook and serve

1. Bring a large pot of salted water to a boil. Add the pasta and simmer for 4 to 5 minutes, until the francobolli float to the surface. Gently remove the pasta with a skimmer or slotted spoon and shake out the excess water.

2. Serve the pasta with the Arugula and Almond Pesto.

Ingredient tip: Use any combination of olives you like. I like pimiento-stuffed green olives and kalamata olives.

SUN-DRIED TOMATO AND BASIL QUADRUCCI

SERVES 4

PREP TIME: 1 hour 20 minutes | **REST TIME:** 30 minutes | **COOK TIME:** 10 minutes

NUT-FREE

QUADRUCCI ARE LITTLE pasta squares. I prefer to use smaller shapes for rich fillings like this one, which has the strong flavor of sun-dried tomatoes. You can seal and cut these by hand, but there are small ravioli stamps and molds available that will help you make these smaller squares faster.

For the filling

1 cup whole milk ricotta

1 cup sun-dried tomatoes packed in oil, drained

5 or 6 fresh basil leaves

Salt

Freshly ground black pepper

2 tablespoons extra-virgin olive oil

½ cup shredded mozzarella cheese

For the pasta

Tipo "00" flour or all-purpose flour, for dusting

1 batch green Flavored Pasta Dough (page 28), made with basil

For serving

Salt

Extra-virgin olive oil, for drizzling

Grated Parmesan cheese

To make the filling

1. In a food processor, combine the ricotta, sun-dried tomatoes, and basil and season with salt and pepper. Turn on the food processor and slowly drizzle in the oil. Process for 2 to 3 minutes, until the tomatoes are finely minced, stopping once to scrape down the sides of the bowl about halfway through.

2. Remove the blade and stir in the mozzarella until combined.

To make the pasta

1. Dust a baking sheet with flour.

2. Using a rolling pin or pasta machine roller, thin one-fourth of the dough into a sheet until you can just barely see your fingers through the pasta, as described on pages 12 to 14. Cut the sheet in half.

3. Dust a clean work surface with flour and lay one of the half-sheets on it. Spoon or pipe the filling onto the sheet in ½-teaspoon dollops, spaced 1 inch apart on all sides (see page 14).

4. Lay the other half pasta sheet on top and gently press it down around the filling to seal the quadrucci and remove any air bubbles. Using a pastry cutter, stamp, or knife, cut the filled pockets into squares. Place the quadrucci on the prepared baking sheet until you are ready to cook.

5. Repeat with the remaining dough and filling.

To cook and serve

1. Bring a large pot of salted water to a boil. Add the pasta and simmer for 4 to 5 minutes, until the quadrucci float to the surface. Gently remove the pasta with a skimmer or slotted spoon and shake out the excess water.

2. Drizzle with oil and top with Parmesan.

MUFFULETTA BOTTLE CAPS WITH CREAMY SUN-DRIED TOMATO SAUCE

SERVES 4

PREP TIME: 1 hour 20 minutes | **REST TIME:** 30 minutes | **COOK TIME:** 10 minutes

A MUFFULETTA IS a famous New Orleans sandwich filled with Italian meats and olives. We make this muffuletta filling at Melina's Fresh Pasta every February to celebrate Mardi Gras. Once, while making tiny round ravioli called anolini, I forgot my little pasta stamp. I found that a deep metal bottle cap was the perfect size to stamp out the stuffed circles. Screw-top caps from soda, liquor, or wine bottles work best. While you have the bottle cap off, you can also make yourself a drink to accompany your pasta in true New Orleans style.

For the filling

1 cup chopped Genoa salami

1 cup chopped mortadella

1 cup shredded pro-volone cheese

½ cup whole milk ricotta cheese

¼ cup muffuletta olive mix (see tip)

For the pasta

Tipo "00" flour or all-purpose flour, for dusting

1 batch Traditional Egg Pasta Dough (page 20)

For serving

Salt

1 batch Creamy Sun-Dried Tomato Sauce (page 110), warmed

To make the filling

1. In a food processor, combine the salami, mortadella, provolone, ricotta, and olive mix. Process until the meats are finely minced. Spoon the mixture into a piping bag, or spoon it into a zip-top bag and cut off a bottom corner. Set aside.

To make the pasta

1. Dust a baking sheet with flour.

2. Using a rolling pin or pasta machine roller, thin one-fourth of the dough into a sheet until you can just barely see your fingers through the pasta, as described on pages 12 to 14. Cut the sheet in half.

3. Dust a clean work surface with flour and lay one of the half-sheets on it. Spoon or pipe the filling onto the sheet in ½-teaspoon dollops, spaced 1 inch apart on all sides (see page 14).

4. Lay the other half pasta sheet on top, and gently press it down around the filling to seal the pasta and remove any air bubbles. Center a bottle cap over the filling and press down firmly to cut and seal the pasta around the filling. Place the pasta on the prepared baking sheet until you are ready to cook.

5. Repeat with the remaining dough and filling.

To cook and serve

1. Bring a large pot of salted water to a boil. Add the pasta and simmer for 4 to 5 minutes, until the bottle caps float to the surface. Gently remove with a skimmer or slotted spoon and shake out the excess water.

2. Serve the pasta with the warmed Creamy Sun-Dried Tomato Sauce.

Ingredient tip: I use a jarred, premade muffuletta olive mix/salad for this recipe. If you cannot find something similar, blend ½ cup pitted olives with ½ carrot and 1 or 2 hot red cherry peppers to mimic the flavors.

ROASTED RED PEPPER AND FRESH MOZZARELLA RAVIOLI WITH ITALIAN SAUSAGE RAGÙ

SERVES 4

PREP TIME: 1 hour 20 minutes | **REST TIME:** 30 minutes | **COOK TIME:** 10 minutes

ROASTED RED PEPPERS are a classic Italian antipasto ingredient. Here, we puree the sweet and smoky peppers with ricotta and fresh mozzarella. Make sure to squeeze the liquid out of the red peppers to get them as dry as possible, or the filling will be too runny to hold its shape. The grated cheese will help to dry out the filling, but you can also add 1 to 2 tablespoons panko bread crumbs if the filling is too runny.

For the filling

2 cups whole milk ricotta

1 (12-ounce) jar roasted red peppers, drained and squeezed dry

½ cup grated Pecorino Romano

Salt

Freshly ground black pepper

1 cup diced fresh mozzarella cheese

For the pasta

Tipo "00" flour or all-purpose flour, for dusting

1 batch herbed Flavored Pasta Dough (page 28), made with dried oregano

For serving

Salt

1 batch Italian Sausage Ragù (page 111), warmed

To make the filling

1. In a food processor, combine the ricotta, roasted red peppers, and Pecorino Romano and season with salt and pepper. Process for 2 to 3 minutes, until smooth, stopping once to scrape down the sides of the bowl about halfway through.

2. Remove the blade and stir in the mozzarella.

To make the pasta

1. Dust a baking sheet with flour.

2. Using a rolling pin or pasta machine roller, thin one-fourth of the dough into a sheet until you can just barely see your fingers through the pasta, as described on pages 12 to 14.

3. Dust a clean work surface with flour and lay the pasta sheet on it. Use a knife to cut the pasta into 3-by-2-inch rectangles.

4. Spoon or pipe 1 tablespoon of filling onto the bottom third of each rectangle. Fold the top half of the rectangles over the filling. Use the tines of a fork to seal the edges securely on the three open sides. Place the pasta on the prepared baking sheet until you are ready to cook.

5. Repeat with the remaining dough and filling.

To cook and serve

1. Bring a large pot of salted water to a boil. Add the pasta and simmer for 4 to 5 minutes, until the ravioli float to the surface. Gently remove the pasta with a skimmer or slotted spoon and shake out the excess water.

2. Serve the pasta with the warmed ragù.

Variation tip: If you prefer, use a picante provolone cheese as a substitute for the mozzarella for a sharper taste.

PISTACHIO AND LEMON DOPPIO RAVIOLI

SERVES 4

PREP TIME: 1 hour 20 minutes | **COOK TIME:** 10 minutes

GLUTEN-FREE

DOPPIO RAVIOLI ARE large, square ravioli made up of two separately sealed sides of different but complimentary fillings. Pistachios are one of my favorite ingredients for fillings, pesto-type sauces, or just as a simple topping to any pasta along with some good extra-virgin olive oil. The pistachio filling is paired with Melina's Fresh Pasta's (almost) famous lemon-ricotta filling.

For the pistachio filling

1 cup shelled, roasted, and salted pistachios

1 cup tightly packed fresh spinach leaves

1 cup tightly packed arugula

1 cup whole milk ricotta cheese

Salt

Freshly ground black pepper

For the lemon filling

1 cup whole milk ricotta cheese

¼ cup grated Parmesan cheese

Grated zest of 1 lemon

1 tablespoon minced fresh parsley

Salt

Freshly ground black pepper

For the pasta

Gluten-free flour blend, for dusting

1 batch Gluten-Free Pasta Dough (page 26)

For serving

Salt

4 tablespoons (½ stick) salted butter

¼ cup grated Parmesan cheese

To make the fillings

1. In a food processor, pulse the pistachios until finely chopped. Add the spinach, arugula, and ricotta and season with salt and pepper. Process until smooth. Scoop the filling into a pastry bag, and set aside.

2. In a clean food processor bowl, combine the ricotta, Parmesan, lemon zest, and parsley and season with salt and pepper. Process until smooth. Alternatively, combine these ingredients in a large bowl and stir until fully blended. Scoop the filling into a pastry bag, and aside.

To make the pasta

1. Dust a baking sheet with flour.

2. Using a rolling pin or pasta machine roller, thin one-fourth of the dough into a sheet until you can just barely see your fingers through the pasta, as described on pages 12 to 14. Cut the sheet in half.

3. Dust a clean work surface with flour and lay one pasta sheet on it.

4. Starting at least ½ inch from the edge of the dough, pipe parallel, 2-inch-long strips of each filling, alternating between the two to create pairs of filling strips like equals signs. Place the strips about ¼ inch apart from each other and leave 1 inch between each filling pair (see page 17).

5. Lay the other pasta sheet on top, and gently press it down around the fillings to seal and remove any air bubbles. Use a thin (⅛-inch) dowel or skewer to tightly press and seal the pasta in the spaces between the filling pairs and across the top, bottom, and at each end of the pasta sheets. Seal, but do not cut through, the pasta.

6. Use a fluted pastry cutter to cut rectangles between the pairs of filling. Place the ravioli on the prepared baking sheet until you are ready to cook.

7. Repeat with the remaining dough and fillings.

To cook and serve

1. Bring a large pot of salted water to a boil. Add the pasta and simmer for 4 to 5 minutes, until the doppio ravioli float to the surface. Gently remove the pasta with a skimmer or slotted spoon and shake out the excess water. Reserve ¼ cup of cooking water.

2. In a large skillet or sauté pan over low heat, melt the butter. Add the Parmesan and reserved cooking water to the pan, and stir to combine.

3. Turn off the heat, add the ravioli, and stir to coat.

CHOCOLATE CANNOLI RAVIOLI WITH RASPBERRY DRIZZLE

SERVES 4

PREP TIME: 1 hour 20 minutes | **REST TIME:** 30 minutes | **COOK TIME:** 35 minutes

NUT-FREE, VEGETARIAN

THIS DESSERT RAVIOLI is made with a chocolate dough and stuffed with home-made cannoli filling. I recommend using a mold for these ravioli so they are well sealed and consistent in size and shape.

For the filling

1 cup whole
milk ricotta

½ cup confection-
ers' sugar

⅛ teaspoon
vanilla extract

⅛ teaspoon ground
cinnamon

1 to 2 tablespoons
mini chocolate chips

Salt

For the pasta

Tipo "00" flour or
all-purpose flour,
for dusting

1 batch chocolate
Flavored Pasta
Dough (page 28),
made with
cocoa powder

For the sauce

6 ounces fresh
raspberries

1 tablespoon granu-
lated sugar

1 tablespoon water,
plus more as needed

2 teaspoons
freshly squeezed
lemon juice

Canola oil, for frying

To make the filling

1. In a large bowl, stir together the ricotta, confectioners' sugar, vanilla, cinnamon, and chocolate chips and season with salt. Scoop the filling into a pastry bag, or spoon it into a zip-top bag and cut off a bottom corner. Set aside.

To make the pasta

1. Dust a baking sheet with flour.

2. Using a rolling pin or pasta machine roller, thin one-fourth of the dough into a sheet until you can just barely see your fingers through the pasta, as described on pages 12 to 14. Cut the sheet in half.

3. Rub flour on one side of one pasta sheet, then lay it on top of a ravioli mold, floured-side down. Use the press to make pockets in the sheet, then spoon or pipe about 1 tablespoon of filling into each of the pockets.

4. Lay the second pasta sheet on top and stretch it to cover the bottom sheet. Use a rolling pin to cut and seal the ravioli by rolling it over the mold in every direction. Remove the excess dough around the mold, and flip the mold over to release the ravioli. Place the ravioli on the prepared baking sheet until you are ready to cook.

5. Repeat with the remaining dough and filling.

To make the sauce

1. In a small saucepan over medium heat, combine the raspberries, granulated sugar, water, and lemon juice. Cook for 6 to 7 minutes, stirring frequently, until the sugar dissolves and the raspberries break down. Remove the pan from the heat, and strain the raspberries through a fine-mesh strainer set over a small bowl to remove the seeds.

To cook and serve

1. Pour enough oil into a large pot or deep-fryer over medium heat to reach a depth of 2 inches. Heat until a frying thermometer registers 375°F.

2. Working in batches, fry the ravioli for 2 minutes or until golden brown, turning them once about halfway through. Transfer to paper towels to drain, and keep warm until you are ready to serve. Repeat with the remaining ravioli.

3. Drizzle the ravioli with raspberry sauce.

Cooking tip: If you don't want to bother with frying, these ravioli are also delicious baked or air fried, but they do tend to pop open and leak out the filling. Bake or air fry at 350°F for 5 minutes.

GOAT CHEESE SPOJA LORDA IN BRODO

SERVES 4

PREP TIME: 1 hour 20 minutes | **REST TIME:** 30 minutes | **COOK TIME:** 10 minutes

NUT-FREE

THIS PASTA IS yet another example of the frugality of Italian cooking that somehow still results in something delicious. *Spoja lorda*, meaning "dirty dough," was designed to use leftover pasta dough scraps and filling from making tortellini. These thin little pasta diamonds are typically served in a broth. I used goat cheese in this recipe as a substitute for squacquerone cheese—the tangy local cheese traditionally used, which is difficult to find outside of Italy.

For the filling

1½ cups whole milk ricotta

½ cup goat cheese, at room temperature

Salt

Freshly ground black pepper

For the pasta

Tipo "00" flour or all-purpose flour, for dusting

1 batch Traditional Egg Pasta Dough (page 20)

For serving

1 batch Parmesan Brodo (page 96)

Grated Parmesan cheese, for serving

To make the filling

1. In a large bowl, stir together the ricotta and goat cheese. Season with salt and pepper and stir again until thoroughly combined.

To make the pasta

1. Dust a baking sheet with flour.

2. Using a rolling pin or pasta machine roller, thin one-fourth of the dough into a sheet until you can just barely see your fingers through the pasta as described on pages 12 to 14. Cut the sheet in half.

3. Dust a clean work surface with flour and lay one of the half-sheets on it. Using a spatula, spread a thin (⅛ inch) layer of the filling across the entire pasta sheet, leaving a ¼-inch border around the edges.

4. Lay the other half pasta sheet on top and gently press the sides of the sheets together to seal.

5. Using a fluted pastry cutter, cut the dough horizontally into long, 1-inch-thick strips. Then, cut diagonally across the dough in the other direction to produce 1-inch diamond shapes. Place the pasta on the prepared baking sheet until you are ready to cook.

6. Repeat with the remaining dough and filling.

To cook and serve

1. In a large pot, bring the brodo to a boil. Add the pasta and simmer for 4 to 5 minutes, until the spoja lorda float to the surface. You may need to cook them in two batches, dividing the brodo in half.

2. Ladle the pasta and some brodo into bowls, top with Parmesan, and serve.

Variation tip: Boil the pasta in salted water instead of broth. Drain, and serve topped with Arugula and Almond Pesto (page 109).

CASONCELLI IN PANCETTA SAGE SAUCE

SERVES 4–6

PREP TIME: 1 hour 20 minutes | **REST TIME:** 30 minutes | **COOK TIME:** 20 minutes

THERE IS ABSOLUTELY zero agreement on what a proper casoncelli filing or shape should be. Casoncelli from Bergamo differ from Casoncelli from Bescia—and these two cities are only 40 minutes apart. I chose this version of filling because it has elements of both. The most common way to shape the stuffed pasta is in a U shape. The pancetta sage sauce is the traditional topping.

For the filling

1 tablespoon
salted butter

2 sweet Italian
sausage links,
casings removed

8 ounces
ground beef

¼ cup golden raisins

1 pear, peeled,
cored, and shredded

½ cup (2 ounces)
amaretti cookies,
crushed into crumbs

2 tablespoons panko
bread crumbs

1 large egg

¼ cup grated Par-
mesan cheese, plus
more for serving

1 tablespoon
chopped
fresh parsley

Dash freshly grated
or ground nutmeg

Salt

Freshly ground
black pepper

For the pasta

Tipo "00" flour or
all-purpose flour,
for dusting

1 batch Traditional
Egg Pasta Dough
(page 20)

For serving

Salt

4 tablespoons
(½ stick)
salted butter

½ cup diced
pancetta

2 fresh sage leaves

To make the filling

1. In a large skillet or sauté pan over medium heat, melt the butter. Add the sausage and ground beef and cook for 8 to 10 minutes, until browned, breaking up the meat with a wooden spoon while it cooks. Stir in the raisins and pear and cook for about 2 minutes, until the liquid cooks off and the filling is dry. Let cool completely.

2. In a large bowl, combine the cooked meat filling, amaretti crumbs, panko bread crumbs, egg, Parmesan, parsley, nutmeg, and salt and pepper to taste. Stir until thoroughly combined.

To make the pasta

1. Dust a baking sheet with flour.

2. Using a rolling pin or pasta machine roller, thin one-fourth of the dough into a sheet until you can just barely see your fingers through the pasta, as described on pages 12 to 14.

3. Dust a clean work surface with flour and lay one pasta sheet on it. Use a 3-inch round ravioli stamp, cookie cutter, or large drinking glass to cut circles from the dough.

4. Place 1 rounded tablespoon of filling ¼ inch from the edge of each circle. Fold the circles in half over the filling, making half-moon shapes. Use your fingers to seal the edges securely. Grab each end of a semicircle with your thumb and forefinger of each hand, and pull the sides toward each other, using your thumbs to make a small indentation in the center of the pasta and forming it into a U shape. Place the pasta on the prepared baking sheet until you are ready to cook.

5. Repeat with the remaining dough and filling.

To cook and serve

1. Bring a large pot of salted water to a boil. Add the pasta and simmer for 4 to 5 minutes, until the casoncelli float to the surface. Gently remove the pasta with a skimmer or slotted spoon and shake out the excess water.

2. In a large skillet or sauté pan over medium heat, melt the butter. Add the pancetta and sage leaves and cook for 4 to 5 minutes, until the pancetta is browned.

3. Add the pasta to the pan and stir gently to coat with the sauce before serving.

MEAT TORTELLINI IN BRODO

SERVES 4

PREP TIME: 1 hour 20 minutes | **REST TIME:** 30 minutes | **COOK TIME:** 40 minutes

IN BOLOGNA, PEOPLE are very particular about their food and recipes. The official recipe for what is allowed in tortellini is registered with the Bologna Chamber of Commerce. The recipe here has all the allowable components, but the ratios are mine, and every family has its own version. You can wander around the *pastificio* (pasta shops) all over Bologna and watch the pasta makers turn out thousands of teeny tiny tortellini, about 1 inch in size, with this traditional meat filling.

For the filling

2 tablespoons salted butter

¼ pound pork loin chops

Salt

Freshly ground black pepper

½ cup minced onion

½ cup minced celery

½ cup minced carrot

½ cup diced mortadella

½ cup diced prosciutto

1 large egg

¼ cup grated Parmesan cheese

For the pasta

Tipo "00" flour or all-purpose flour, for dusting

1 batch Traditional Egg Pasta Dough (page 20)

For serving

1 batch Parmesan Brodo (page 96)

Parmesan cheese

To make the filling

1. In a large skillet or sauté pan over medium heat, heat the butter until melted. Add the pork loin chop and season with salt and pepper. Cook for 8 to 10 minutes, until browned. Let cool completely, then dice the meat.

2. Add the onion, celery, and carrot to the same pan and cook for 5 to 6 minutes, until the vegetables are soft and any liquid cooks off.

3. Add the mortadella and prosciutto and cook for 3 to 4 minutes, until the meats are slightly browned.

4. Transfer the cooled meat mixture to a food processor, add the egg and Parmesan, and process until a thick paste forms.

To make the pasta

1. Dust a baking sheet with flour.

2. Using a rolling pin or pasta machine roller, thin one-fourth of the dough into a sheet until you can just barely see your fingers through the pasta as described on pages 12 to 14.

3. Dust a clean work surface with flour and lay the pasta sheet on it. Use a knife to cut the pasta into 2-inch squares.

4. Spoon ¼ teaspoon of filling just above one corner of each square. Fold the top half of the pasta squares over the filling to form triangles. Use your fingers to seal the edges securely. Pull the bottom corners of the triangles down toward each other and pinch to seal. Place the pasta on the prepared baking sheet until you are ready to cook.

5. Repeat with the remaining dough and filling.

To cook and serve

1. In a large pot, bring the brodo to a boil. Add the pasta and simmer for 4 to 5 minutes, until the tortellini float to the surface. You may need to cook this in two batches, dividing the brodo in half.

2. Ladle the tortellini and some brodo into bowls, top with Parmesan, and serve.

Ingredient tips: You can find diced prosciutto in the deli section of your grocery store, or you can have the deli cut ¼-inch-thick slices for you, which will be easier to dice for this recipe. While pork loin is traditional, you can substitute ground pork to simplify the process—just don't tell your Italian friends!

BAKED CHICKEN CAPPELLETTI IN THREE-CHEESE SAUCE

SERVES 4

PREP TIME: 1 hour 20 minutes | **REST TIME:** 30 minutes | **COOK TIME:** 55 minutes

NUT-FREE

ASK 10 ITALIANS the difference between tortellini and cappelletti, and you'll get 10 different answers on the filling, shape, and how they are served. The most agreed-upon version attributes the pork-filled tortellini as coming from Emilia and the cheese and chicken–filled cappelletti coming from the other half of the region, Romagna. These cappelletti are a good alternative for those who do not eat pork.

For the filling

2 tablespoons salted butter

½ cup minced onion

½ cup minced celery

½ cup minced carrot

1 garlic clove, minced

1 pound ground chicken

1 tablespoon minced fresh rosemary

Salt

Freshly ground black pepper

¼ cup grated Parmesan cheese

1 large egg

For the pasta

Tipo "00" flour or all-purpose flour, for dusting

1 batch Traditional Egg Pasta Dough (page 20)

For serving

Salt

Three-Cheese Sauce (page 108)

2 tablespoons panko bread crumbs

2 tablespoons grated Parmesan cheese

To make the filling

1. In a large skillet over medium heat, melt the butter. Add the onion, celery, carrot, and garlic and cook for 6 to 8 minutes, until the vegetables are soft.

2. Add the ground chicken and rosemary and season with salt and pepper. Cook for 8 to 10 minutes, until the chicken is browned, breaking up the meat with a wooden spoon while it cooks. Let cool completely.

3. In a food processor, combine the cooled chicken mixture, Parmesan, and egg. Process until a thick paste forms.

To make the pasta

1. Dust a baking sheet with flour.

2. Using a rolling pin or pasta machine roller, thin one-fourth of the dough into a sheet until you can just barely see your fingers through the pasta, as described on pages 12 to 14.

3. Dust a clean work surface with flour and lay the pasta sheet on it. Using a 2-inch glass or a round ravioli stamp, cut the dough into circles.

4. Spoon ¼ teaspoon of filling onto the bottom half of each circle. Fold the top half of the circles over the filling to form half-moons. Use your fingers to seal the edges securely. Pull the bottom corners of the half-moons toward each other and pinch to seal. Place the cappelletti on the prepared baking sheet until you are ready to cook.

5. Repeat with the remaining dough and filling.

To cook and serve

1. Preheat the oven to 375°F.

2. Bring a large pot of salted water to a boil. Add the pasta and simmer for 4 to 5 minutes. Gently remove the cappelletti with a skimmer or slotted spoon and shake out the excess water. Reserve ¼ cup of the pasta cooking water. The pasta may be slightly undercooked at this point, but will finish cooking in the oven.

3. In a small saucepan over medium heat, cook the Three-Cheese Sauce for about 5 minutes until warmed. Turn off the heat and stir in the reserved pasta water to combine. Coat the bottom of a 9-by-13-inch baking pan with one-fourth of the cheese sauce. Add the cappelletti to the pan. Pour the remaining sauce over the pasta. Top with the panko bread crumbs and Parmesan.

4. Bake for 20 to 25 minutes, until the sauce is bubbling and the top begins to brown.

MUSHROOM CAPPELLACCI WITH FRESH CHERRY TOMATO SAUCE

SERVES 2

PREP TIME: 1 hour 20 minutes | **REST TIME:** 30 minutes | **COOK TIME:** 30 minutes

DAIRY-FREE, NUT-FREE, VEGAN

USE YOUR FAVORITE mushroom combination here—button and cremini (a.k.a. baby bella) work well, but you can add any fresh mushrooms you like, including shiitake and oyster. Cappellacci, shaped to resemble little hats, look similar to tortellini but are larger.

For the filling

1 pound mixed fresh mushrooms

2 tablespoons extra-virgin olive oil

¼ cup minced shallot

2 teaspoons fresh thyme leaves

Salt

Freshly ground black pepper

¼ cup dry white wine

2 tablespoons balsamic vinegar

For the pasta

Tipo "00" flour or all-purpose flour, for dusting

1 batch Eggless Pasta Dough (page 22)

For serving

Salt

1 batch Fresh Cherry Tomato Sauce (page 106), warmed

Make the filling

1. In a food processor, pulse the mushrooms until finely chopped.

2. Coat the bottom of a large skillet or sauté pan over medium heat with the oil. Add the shallot and sauté for 2 to 3 minutes, until it is soft.

3. Add the chopped mushrooms and thyme and season with salt and pepper. Cook for about 4 minutes, until the mushrooms begin to soften.

4. Pour in the wine, increase the heat to medium-high, and cook for 5 to 6 minutes, until all of the liquid is evaporated, stirring often so the mushrooms do not stick.

5. Stir in the vinegar and cook for 2 to 3 minutes, until all liquid evaporates and the mushrooms are dry. Turn off the heat and let the mushrooms cool.

To make the pasta

1. Dust a baking sheet with flour.

2. Using a rolling pin or pasta machine roller, thin one-fourth of the dough into a sheet until you can just barely see your fingers through the pasta, as described on pages 12 to 14.

3. Dust a clean work surface with flour and lay the pasta sheet on it. Use a knife to cut the pasta into 3-inch squares.

4. Place 1 rounded tablespoon of mushrooms near one corner of each square. Fold the top half of each square over the filling to form triangles. Use your fingers to seal the edges securely. Pull the triangle corners down toward each other into a point and pinch to seal. Place the cappellacci on the prepared baking sheet until you are ready to cook.

5. Repeat with the remaining dough and filling.

To cook and serve

1. Bring a large pot of salted water to a boil. Add the pasta and simmer for 4 to 5 minutes, until the cappellacci float to the surface. Gently remove the pasta with a skimmer or slotted spoon and shake out the excess water.

2. Serve the pasta with the Fresh Cherry Tomato Sauce.

Cooking tip: Make sure the mushrooms are cooked until they are dry so the filling holds its shape. If you prefer a creamier—though not vegan—filling, stir ½ cup whole milk ricotta into the cooked mushrooms.

ASPARAGUS MASCARPONE TORTELLONI

SERVES 4

PREP TIME: 1 hour 20 minutes | **REST TIME:** 30 minutes | **COOK TIME:** 10 minutes

NUT-FREE

TORTELLONI ARE LARGER versions of little ring-shaped tortellini. I chose this shape for the larger filling pocket, so the pasta can hold more of the delicious filling. Mascarpone is a slightly sweet, buttery-tasting, soft Italian cheese, similar to cream cheese in consistency, which counters the slightly bitter asparagus flavor in this rich filling. You can find mascarpone in tubs in the cheese sections of most grocery stores.

For the filling

2 cups whole milk ricotta

1 cup mascarpone cheese

1 pound asparagus, tough ends trimmed, chopped into 1-inch pieces, tips reserved

½ cup grated Parmesan cheese

Salt

Freshly ground black pepper

For the pasta

Tipo "00" flour or all-purpose flour, for dusting

1 batch Traditional Egg Pasta Dough (page 20)

For serving

Salt

2 tablespoons extra-virgin olive oil, plus more for drizzling

Freshly ground black pepper

To make the filling

1. In a food processor, combine the ricotta, mascarpone, asparagus (minus the reserved tips), and Parmesan and process until the ingredients are mixed well and the asparagus is finely minced. Taste and season with salt and pepper.

To make the pasta

1. Dust a baking sheet with flour.

2. Using a rolling pin or pasta machine roller, thin one-fourth of the dough into a sheet until you can just barely see your fingers through the pasta, as described on pages 12 to 14.

3. Dust a clean work surface with flour and lay the pasta sheet on it. Use a 3-inch round ravioli stamp, cookie cutter, or large drinking glass to cut the pasta into circles.

4. Place 1 rounded tablespoon of filling ¼ inch from the edge of each circle. Fold the circles in half, making half-moon shapes. Use your fingers to seal the edges securely. Gently wrap the half-moons around your finger and pinch the ends together to seal. Place the tortelloni on the prepared baking sheet until you are ready to cook.

5. Repeat with the remaining dough and filling.

To cook and serve

1. Bring a large pot of salted water to a boil. Add the pasta and simmer for 4 to 5 minutes, until the tortelloni float to the surface. Gently remove the pasta with a skimmer or slotted spoon and shake out the excess water.

2. While the pasta cooks, in a large skillet or sauté pan over medium-high heat, heat the oil. Add the reserved asparagus tips, season with salt and pepper, and cook for 4 to 5 minutes, until the tips are bright green and crisp-tender.

3. Top the tortelloni with the asparagus tips and drizzle with oil.

CARAMELLE ALLA BOLOGNA

SERVES 4

PREP TIME: 1 hour 20 minutes | **REST TIME:** 30 minutes | **COOK TIME:** 10 minutes

THIS FILLING IS a tribute to the food of Bologna, the historic capital of the Emilia-Romagna region in northern Italy. The rich food of the region—Parmigiano-Reggiano cheese, cured meats such as prosciutto di Parma and mortadella, and aged balsamic vinegar—earned Bologna the name *la grassa*, which means "the fat one." *Caramelle* means "candy" in Italian, and these little pasta parcels resemble twisted candy wrappers. The meats and cheeses are salty, so no added seasoning is needed for the filling.

For the filling

1 cup chopped mortadella

1 cup chopped prosciutto

½ cup grated Parmesan cheese, plus more for topping

½ cup whole milk ricotta cheese

For the pasta

Tipo "00" flour or all-purpose flour, for dusting

1 batch Traditional Egg Pasta Dough (page 20)

For serving

Salt

2 tablespoons aged balsamic vinegar, plus more for topping

Grated Parmesan cheese

To make the filling

1. In a food processor, combine the mortadella, prosciutto, Parmesan, and ricotta and process until smooth. Scoop the filling into a pastry bag, or spoon it into a zip-top bag and cut off a bottom corner. Set aside.

To make the pasta

1. Dust a baking sheet with flour.

2. Using a rolling pin or pasta machine roller, thin one-fourth of the dough into a sheet until you can just barely see your fingers through the pasta, as described on pages 12 to 14.

3. Dust a clean work surface with flour and lay the pasta sheet on it. Use a knife to cut the sheet into 3-inch squares.

4. Pipe a 2-inch-long line of filling horizontally on the lower third of each pasta square. Fold the dough over the filling. Create a seal by gently rolling the pasta on the table. Seal the edges by squeezing them shut with your fingers so they are flat, then pinch or twist the edges together. Place the pasta on the prepared baking sheet until you are ready to cook.

5. Repeat with the remaining dough and filling.

To cook and serve

1. Bring a large pot of salted water to a boil. Add the pasta and simmer for 4 to 5 minutes, until the caramelle float to the surface. Gently remove the pasta with a skimmer or slotted spoon and shake out the excess water.

2. Drizzle the caramelle with the vinegar and top with Parmesan.

Cooking tip: The dough needs to be a little wet to seal and twist this shape properly. If needed, dip your finger into water and run it along the outside edges of the dough squares to keep them pliable and ensure a proper seal.

Ingredient tip: Ask the deli counter at your local grocery store to cut ¼-inch-thick slabs of mortadella and prosciutto for this recipe.

AGNOLOTTI DI MAGRO IN BRODO

SERVES 4

PREP TIME: 1 hour 20 minutes | **REST TIME:** 30 minutes

CHILL TIME: 30 minutes | **COOK TIME:** 10 minutes

NUT-FREE

MAGRO MEANS "THIN" in Italian, and *di magro* is a filling that doesn't contain meat. Agnolotti are little pasta pillows that are pinched to seal. No molds or stamps are needed for this recipe. These stuffed pasta shapes are made with your hands and a fluted pastry cutter. I paired this with a *brodo,* or broth, in which the pasta is cooked directly.

For the filling

1 cup whole milk ricotta

1 cup shredded mozzarella cheese

1 cup grated Parmesan cheese

1 cup panko bread crumbs

⅛ teaspoon freshly grated or ground nutmeg

Salt

Freshly ground black pepper

For the pasta

Whole wheat or all-purpose flour, for dusting

1 batch Whole Wheat Pasta Dough (page 24)

For serving

1 batch Parmesan Brodo (page 96)

Grated Parmesan cheese

To make the filling

1. In a food processor, combine the ricotta, mozzarella, Parmesan, panko bread crumbs, and nutmeg and season with salt and pepper. Process until smooth. Cover and refrigerate for 30 minutes.

2. Scoop the chilled filling into a pastry bag, or spoon it into a zip-top bag and cut a ¾-inch hole in a bottom corner.

To make the pasta

1. Dust a baking sheet with flour.

2. Using a rolling pin or pasta machine roller, thin one-fourth of the dough into a sheet until you can just barely see your fingers through the pasta, as described on pages 12 to 14.

3. Dust a clean work surface with flour and lay the pasta sheet on it.

4. Pipe 1½-inch-long horizontal strips of filling, ½ inch apart, in a straight line across the lower third of the pasta sheet. Roll the top part of the dough over the filling to form a tube of filling, leaving about 1 inch of dough in front of the filling overlapping the bottom sheet. Press the edges to seal the dough.

5. Using your fingers, pinch the dough together between the filling strips to seal the sides of the tube into individual pockets of filling and to remove as much air as possible (see page 14).

6. Trim the bottom edge of the overlapping dough with the fluted pastry cutter, leaving about ½ inch of dough in front of the filling. Then, cut at each pinch, moving the fluted pastry cutter away from you, which will form a pillow of pasta with pinched edges (see page 18). Place the pasta on the prepared baking sheet until you are ready to cook.

7. Repeat with the remaining dough and filling.

To cook and serve

1. In a large pot, bring the brodo to a boil. Add the pasta and simmer for 4 to 5 minutes, until the agnolotti float to the surface. You may need to cook this in two batches, dividing the brodo in half.

2. Ladle the agnolotti and some brodo into bowls, top with Parmesan, and serve.

PEAR AND GORGONZOLA SACCHETTINI WITH BROWNED BUTTER AND PROSCIUTTO

SERVES 4

PREP TIME: 1 hour 20 minutes | **CHILL TIME:** 1 hour
REST TIME: 30 minutes | **COOK TIME:** 15 minutes

NUT-FREE

SACCHETTINI, ALSO KNOWN as beggar's purses, are little filled pasta pouches. The pouches are twisted and fastened at the top to resemble a small sack. These sweet and salty ravioli are perfect with a simple brown butter sauce and a topping of crispy prosciutto. Because the filling needs to be chilled before it can be placed onto the pasta dough, make the filling before the dough to give it time to firm up.

For the filling

2 pears, peeled and cored

1 cup whole milk ricotta cheese

½ cup (4 ounces) Gorgonzola cheese

Salt

Freshly ground black pepper

For the pasta

Tipo "00" flour or all-purpose flour, for dusting

1 batch Traditional Egg Pasta Dough (page 20)

For serving

Salt

4 prosciutto slices

4 tablespoons (½ stick) salted butter

To make the filling

1. Grate the pear using the large holes of a box grater. Squeeze out as much liquid as you can, and place the pear in a large bowl. You should have about 3 cups.

2. Add the ricotta and Gorgonzola and season with salt and pepper. Stir until thoroughly combined. Refrigerate for 1 hour while you make the pasta.

To make the pasta

1. Dust a baking sheet with flour.

2. Using a rolling pin or pasta machine roller, thin one-fourth of the dough into a sheet until you can just barely see your fingers through the pasta, as described on pages 12 to 14.

3. Dust a clean work surface with flour and lay the pasta sheet on it. Use a knife to cut the pasta into 3-inch squares.

4. Place 1 tablespoon of filling into the center of each square. Dip your finger in water and run it along the edges of the pasta squares to dampen them slightly. The pasta needs to be sticky to hold this shape.

5. Gather the dough up around the filling, then tightly pinch it closed about ¼ inch from the top. Be careful not to tear the pasta. (You might need a few practice purses.) Place the pasta on the prepared baking sheet until you are ready to cook.

6. Repeat with the remaining dough and filling.

To cook and serve

1. Bring a large pot of salted water to a boil. Use a spoon to carefully lower the pasta into the water. Simmer for 4 to 5 minutes, until the sacchettini float to the surface. Gently remove the pasta with a skimmer or slotted spoon and shake out the excess water.

2. While the pasta cooks, in a large skillet or sauté pan over medium-low heat, slowly cook the prosciutto for 4 to 5 minutes, turning, until it is crispy on both sides. Remove the prosciutto from the skillet, then crumble it or cut it into slices.

3. Increase the heat under the skillet to medium, add the butter, and cook until it starts to foam. Turn the heat to low and cook the butter for 4 to 5 minutes, stirring frequently, until light-brown specks begin to form in the skillet. Turn off the heat.

4. Add the cooked pasta to the skillet and gently stir to coat in the browned butter. Top with the crispy prosciutto and serve.

'NDUJA AND BURRATA TRIANGLES WITH NO-COOK TOMATO
AND CASTELVETRANO OLIVE SAUCE · 52

CHAPTER FOUR

SAUCES

ALTHOUGH STUFFED PASTA can be enjoyed with just a glug of extra-virgin olive oil and a dusting of grated Parmesan cheese, the sauces in this chapter—which include tomato, cream, cheese, and meat sauces—pair well with many of the fillings in this book. It is a good idea to get the sauce cooking before you make the pasta, so it can simmer while you form the stuffed pastas. There are some sauces that don't even need to be cooked, but making them ahead of the pasta provides extra time for the flavors to meld before serving.

PARMESAN BRODO

MAKES 4 CUPS, ENOUGH TO SERVE 4

PREP TIME: 20 minutes | COOK TIME: 2 hours 30 minutes

GLUTEN-FREE, NUT-FREE

YOU CAN FIND Parmesan rinds in the cheese section of your grocery store if you aren't saving your own in the freezer. This broth will be used as a substitute for water when cooking some of the stuffed pasta in this book and will be served with the pasta.

2 tablespoons extra-virgin olive oil

1 small onion, unpeeled and halved lengthwise

1 head garlic, halved

5 cups water

2 carrots, unpeeled and halved

8 ounces Parmesan cheese rinds

1 teaspoon whole peppercorns

1 bay leaf

1. Coat the bottom of a large nonstick stockpot over medium heat with the oil. Place the onion and garlic, cut-side down, in the pot and let them brown for 3 to 4 minutes.

2. Add the water, carrots, Parmesan rinds, peppercorns, and bay leaf to the pot. Increase the heat to medium-high and bring to a boil. Reduce the heat to low, cover the pot, and simmer for 2½ hours, stirring frequently so the cheese doesn't stick to the bottom of the pot.

3. Place a fine-mesh strainer over a large heatproof bowl and strain the broth in it. Discard the solids.

4. Transfer the broth to an airtight container; refrigerate for up to 3 days or freeze for up to 3 months.

Cooking tip: I recommend using a 4- to 5-quart nonstick stockpot for this recipe to prevent the cheese from sticking to the bottom of the pot.

CLASSIC MARINARA SAUCE

MAKES 3 CUPS, ENOUGH TO SERVE 4

PREP TIME: 10 minutes | **COOK TIME:** 25 minutes

DAIRY-FREE, GLUTEN-FREE, NUT-FREE, VEGAN

MARINARA SAUCE IS a simple, quick-cooked sauce that features flavorful tomatoes. Although you can use any tomato from your pantry, you'll get the best results using whole San Marzano–style or plum tomatoes. In this case, I prefer canned tomatoes over fresh because they are already peeled and make for a simple preparation. But you can use fresh tomatoes in season, of course. This sauce can serve as the base for a number of sauces, simply by adding cooked meat, herbs, vegetables, and so forth.

¼ cup extra-virgin olive oil

3 garlic cloves, thinly sliced

Dash red pepper flakes (optional)

1 (28-ounce) can San Marzano–style tomatoes or whole plum tomatoes, undrained

Salt

Freshly ground black pepper

2 tablespoons chopped fresh basil leaves (do not use dried)

1. Coat the bottom of a large shallow skillet or sauté over pan medium heat with the oil. Add the garlic and red pepper flakes (if using) and cook for 3 to 4 minutes, until the garlic is softened, being careful not to brown or burn the garlic.

2. Add the tomatoes and their juices to the skillet, breaking the tomatoes into smaller pieces with a wooden spoon. Season with salt and pepper to taste. Simmer the sauce for about 15 minutes, until it is slightly thickened and some of the liquid has cooked off.

3. Stir in the basil and cook for 5 minutes.

4. Serve over your favorite pasta, or let cool, transfer to an airtight container, and refrigerate for up to 3 days or freeze for up to 3 months.

Cooking tip: A large, shallow skillet is the best choice when preparing this sauce because the larger surface area helps it cook more quickly and evaporate some of the excess liquid from the tomatoes to thicken it.

ROASTED TOMATO AND THYME SAUCE

MAKES 3 CUPS, ENOUGH TO SERVE 4

PREP TIME: 15 minutes | **COOK TIME:** 45 minutes

DAIRY-FREE, GLUTEN-FREE, NUT-FREE, VEGAN

ROASTING TOMATOES IS a great way to make a fresh-tasting sauce with less-than-ripe tomatoes in winter. Roasted tomato sauce has a mild tomato taste and is a perfect accompaniment to those stuffed pastas whose filling flavors you do not want to overwhelm with a strong sauce. Roma or plum tomatoes are preferred, but you can use cherry tomatoes for a slightly sweeter sauce, or any tomato you prefer.

2 pounds plum tomatoes, halved

6 garlic cloves, peeled

1 small sweet onion, quartered

3 tablespoons extra-virgin olive oil, divided

1 teaspoon fresh thyme leaves

Salt

Freshly ground black pepper

1. Preheat the oven to 375°F. Line a large rimmed baking sheet with parchment paper or aluminum foil.

2. In a large bowl, stir together the tomatoes, garlic, onion, and 1 tablespoon of oil and spread the mixture on the prepared baking sheet. Drizzle evenly with the remaining 2 tablespoons of oil, sprinkle with thyme, and season to taste with salt and pepper.

3. Roast for 45 minutes, stirring once or twice, until the tomatoes are soft and just starting to fall apart. Remove and let cool for 10 minutes.

4. Transfer the roasted vegetables to a food processor or blender, or a large bowl if using an immersion blender, and blend to your desired consistency. Taste and season with salt and pepper.

5. Serve over your favorite pasta, or let cool, transfer to an airtight container, and refrigerate for up to 3 days or freeze for up to 3 months.

WHITE BOLOGNESE

MAKES 3 CUPS, ENOUGH TO SERVE 4

PREP TIME: 20 minutes | **COOK TIME:** 1 hour 25 minutes

GLUTEN-FREE, NUT-FREE

A RAGÙ IS a meat-based Italian sauce. Bolognese is a variation of ragù—a meat sauce made with tomatoes. This recipe is yet another variation: a velvety, meaty ragù made without tomatoes. A bit of cream added at the end rounds out the flavors and adds body to the sauce so it coats the pasta. Remember: Bolognese is not a saucy sauce; it is more like a flavorful meat topping.

2 tablespoons extra-virgin olive oil

2 ounces diced pancetta

¼ cup minced onion

¼ cup minced carrot

¼ cup minced celery

8 ounces ground veal or lean beef

8 ounces ground pork

Salt

Freshly ground black pepper

½ cup dry white wine

1 cup beef broth

1 teaspoon minced fresh rosemary leaves

1 teaspoon minced fresh sage leaves

⅛ teaspoon freshly grated or ground nutmeg

¼ cup heavy (whipping) cream

2 tablespoons grated Parmesan cheese

1. Coat the bottom of a large Dutch oven or pot over medium-low heat with the oil. Add the pancetta and sauté for 4 to 5 minutes, until browned.

2. Add the onion, carrot, and celery and sauté for 6 to 8 minutes, until soft.

3. Add the ground veal (or beef) and pork, season with salt and pepper, and cook for 8 to 10 minutes, until the meat is browned.

4. Add the wine, increase the heat to medium-high, and simmer for 8 to 10 minutes, until the wine cooks off.

CONTINUED

5. Pour in the broth and add the rosemary, sage, and nutmeg. Taste and season with salt and pepper as needed. Partially cover the pot, and simmer the sauce for 45 minutes, stirring often, until the liquid is almost entirely evaporated.

6. Stir in the heavy cream and Parmesan and cook, uncovered, for 5 minutes to thicken the sauce further.

7. Serve over your favorite pasta, or let cool, transfer to an airtight container, and refrigerate for up to 3 days or freeze for up to 3 months.

Ingredient tip: Substitute Italian sausage for the ground pork for a zestier flavor.

Cooking tip: Use a few tablespoons of pasta cooking water to thin the sauce if needed when serving.

PESTO CREAM SAUCE

PREP TIME: 15 minutes

GLUTEN-FREE

TRADITIONAL BASIL PESTO originated in Genoa, in the Liguria region of northern Italy, and contains garlic, fresh basil, and pine nuts blended with olive oil and Parmesan cheese. You can tinker with the ingredients any way you choose and use different herb or nut combinations to suit your tastes. This recipe begins with the traditional ingredients but finishes with the addition of cream to make a more luxurious sauce.

2 cups tightly packed fresh basil leaves

1 garlic clove, peeled

¼ cup pine nuts

½ cup grated Parmesan cheese

½ cup extra-virgin olive oil

½ cup heavy (whipping) cream

Salt

Freshly ground black pepper

1. In a food processor or blender, combine the basil, garlic, pine nuts, and Parmesan. Turn on the processor and slowly drizzle in the oil. Blend for 2 to 3 minutes, until smooth, stopping once to scrape down the sides of the bowl about halfway through.

2. Pour the cream into the processor and blend until the sauce is thick and smooth. Taste and season with salt and pepper as needed.

3. Serve over your favorite pasta, or transfer to an airtight container, top the sauce with oil to cover, and refrigerate for up to 3 days or freeze up to 1 month.

MUSHROOM RAGÙ

MAKES 4 CUPS, ENOUGH TO SERVE 4

PREP TIME: 20 minutes | **COOK TIME:** 40 minutes

GLUTEN-FREE, NUT-FREE, VEGETARIAN

THIS RECIPE WAS inspired by my Colgate University classmate Lauren Braun Costello, a trained chef, who can be found online at her blog *It's Lauren, of Course!*, sharing helpful tips for the home cook. This is a meatless version of a traditional ragù, without the hours of traditional simmering time. Use thick, firm mushrooms, such as button, cremini, shiitake, or even fresh porcini, if you can find them.

3 tablespoons extra-virgin olive oil

½ cup chopped onion

½ cup chopped carrot

2 garlic cloves, minced

1½ pounds mushrooms, chopped

½ teaspoon fresh thyme leaves

Salt

Freshly ground black pepper

1 (28-ounce) can crushed tomatoes

¼ cup heavy (whipping) cream

1. Coat the bottom of a large skillet or sauté pan over medium-low heat with the oil. Add the onion, carrot, and garlic and sauté for 4 to 5 minutes, until soft.

2. Add the mushrooms and thyme and season with salt and pepper. Cook for about 5 minutes, until the mushrooms are soft.

3. Add the tomatoes, cover the skillet, and let the mixture simmer for 20 to 30 minutes, stirring often. Remove from the heat and stir in the heavy cream.

4. Serve over your favorite pasta, or let cool, transfer to an airtight container, and refrigerate for up to 3 days or freeze for up to 3 months.

Variation tip: Omit the heavy cream to make this sauce vegan.

SUNDAY SAUCE

MAKES 4 CUPS, ENOUGH TO SERVE 6

PREP TIME: 15 minutes | COOK TIME: 2 hours

DAIRY-FREE, GLUTEN-FREE, NUT-FREE

"SUNDAY SAUCE" IS the term used for the long-simmering tomato-and-meat sauce Nonna made that cooked all morning and was served when everyone gathered for family dinner, which in Italian households is at 2 p.m. sharp on Sundays. This sauce honors that tradition, so gather some friends, family, and wine and serve this lovely sauce over your favorite pasta with the meat alongside as a second course.

2 tablespoons extra-virgin olive oil

1 pound sweet Italian sausage links

½ cup chopped onion

½ cup diced prosciutto

½ pound cooked meatballs (optional)

1 cup red wine

1 (28-ounce) can crushed tomatoes

Salt

Freshly ground black pepper

1. In a large Dutch oven or pot over medium heat, heat the oil. Add the sausage and cook for 8 to 10 minutes, turning, until the meat is browned on all sides. Remove the sausage from the pot and set it aside.

2. Add the onion and the prosciutto to the pot. Using a wooden spoon, scrape up any browned sausage bits stuck to the bottom of the pot. Sauté for 4 to 5 minutes, until the onion is soft.

3. Return the sausage to the pot, add the meatballs (if using), and pour in the wine. Increase the heat to medium-high and cook for 6 to 8 minutes, until half of the wine is evaporated.

4. Reduce the heat to medium, add the tomatoes, and season with salt and pepper. Partially cover the pot and simmer the sauce for 1½ hours, stirring occasionally.

5. Serve over your favorite pasta, or let cool, transfer to an airtight container, and refrigerate for up to 3 days or freeze for up to 3 months.

Ingredient tip: Always cook with a wine you would drink on its own. I would recommend a Sangiovese or Zinfandel for this sauce.

NO-COOK TOMATO AND CASTELVETRANO OLIVE SAUCE

MAKES 4 CUPS, ENOUGH TO SERVE 4

PREP TIME: 15 minutes

DAIRY-FREE, GLUTEN-FREE, NUT-FREE, VEGAN

CASTELVETRANO OLIVES ARE large, green, meaty olives from Sicily with a sweet, buttery taste. They add an extra level of bright, salty flavor to this quick, uncooked tomato sauce. Use a high-quality fruity extra-virgin olive oil because this sauce is raw. This sauce is best during the height of tomato season; use the freshest tomatoes you can find.

½ cup extra-virgin olive oil

2 pounds ripe tomatoes, quartered if large

1 garlic clove, peeled

Salt

Freshly ground black pepper

2 cups Castelvetrano olives, pitted and drained

1. In a food processor, blender, or a large bowl if using an immersion blender, combine the oil, tomatoes, and garlic; blend until smooth. Taste and season with salt and pepper.

2. Add the olives and pulse a few times to chop them, but do not puree.

3. Serve over your favorite pasta, or transfer to an airtight container and refrigerate for up to 3 days or freeze for up to 3 months.

Ingredient tip: Most grocery stores carry Castelvetrano olives, but you can use any pitted olive, such as green Manzanilla or even kalamata—the flavor will not be as delicate, but the sauce will still be delicious.

LEMON CREAM SAUCE

MAKES 1 CUP, ENOUGH TO SERVE 4

PREP TIME: 10 minutes | **COOK TIME:** 20 minutes

GLUTEN-FREE, NUT-FREE

A LITTLE GOES a long way with this rich lemon cream sauce. There is no substitute for freshly squeezed lemon juice and grated lemon zest in this recipe—they are the sources of the lemony goodness.

4 tablespoons (½ stick) salted butter

¼ cup freshly squeezed lemon juice

1 cup heavy (whipping) cream

½ cup grated Parmesan cheese

1 tablespoon grated lemon zest

Salt

Freshly ground black pepper

1. In a small saucepan over low heat, melt the butter. Stir in the lemon juice and cook for 1 minute.

2. Stir in the heavy cream and Parmesan to combine. Increase the heat to medium and cook the sauce for 10 to 15 minutes, until the cream reduces by half, stirring frequently to prevent scalding.

3. Turn off the heat and stir in the lemon zest. Taste and season with salt and pepper.

4. Serve over your favorite pasta, or let cool, transfer to an airtight container, and refrigerate for up to 3 days. This sauce does not freeze well, as it will separate.

FRESH CHERRY TOMATO SAUCE

MAKES 4 CUPS, ENOUGH TO SERVE 4

PREP TIME: 10 minutes | **COOK TIME:** 20 minutes

DAIRY-FREE, GLUTEN-FREE, NUT-FREE, VEGAN

THERE IS NOTHING like a pasta sauce made with fresh, ripe tomatoes. You can make a quick but flavorful sauce with sweet cherry tomatoes—in just a few minutes with just a few ingredients. The secret is using high heat and stirring until the tomatoes burst and release their liquid into the sauce.

¼ cup extra-virgin olive oil

2 garlic cloves, minced

¼ cup chopped onion

2 pints (1¼ pounds) cherry tomatoes

Salt

Freshly ground black pepper

2 tablespoons chopped fresh basil leaves

1. Coat the bottom of a large skillet or sauté pan over medium-low heat with the oil. Add the garlic and onion and sauté for 4 to 5 minutes, until soft.

2. Add the tomatoes, increase the heat to medium-high, and cook for 6 to 8 minutes, stirring often, until the tomatoes are cooked through and begin to burst.

3. Using a wooden spoon, mash and stir the tomatoes as they continue to cook for 4 to 5 minutes more. Taste and season with salt and pepper.

4. Turn off the heat and stir in the basil.

5. Serve over your favorite pasta, or let cool, transfer to an airtight container, and refrigerate for up to 3 days or freeze for up to 3 months.

Variation tip: If you prefer a smooth sauce, use an immersion blender right in the skillet to blend the sauce to your desired consistency.

BEEF, RED BELL PEPPER, AND TOMATO SAUCE

MAKES 4 CUPS, ENOUGH TO SERVE 4

PREP TIME: 10 minutes | COOK TIME: 45 minutes

DAIRY-FREE, GLUTEN-FREE, NUT-FREE

THIS TWIST ON a classic meat sauce adds chopped red bell pepper to mimic the taste of stuffed peppers. It doesn't require hours of simmering time like a traditional ragù, so this sauce is a good option for a quick and flavorful meal when meat sauce is required.

2 tablespoons extra-virgin olive oil

¼ cup minced onion

1 garlic clove, minced

1 cup chopped red bell pepper (1 medium pepper)

1 pound ground beef

Salt

Freshly ground black pepper

1 (28-ounce) can crushed tomatoes

1. Coat the bottom of a large Dutch oven or pot over medium heat with the oil. Add the onion and garlic and sauté for 4 to 5 minutes, until soft.

2. Add the bell pepper and cook for 5 to 6 minutes, until soft.

3. Add the ground beef, season with salt and pepper, and cook for 8 to 10 minutes, until the meat is browned.

4. Stir in the tomatoes, partially cover the pot, and simmer the sauce for 30 minutes, stirring often.

5. Serve with your favorite pasta, or let cool, transfer to an airtight container, and refrigerate for up to 3 days or freeze for up to 3 months.

THREE-CHEESE SAUCE

MAKES 2 CUPS, ENOUGH TO SERVE 4

PREP TIME: 20 minutes | **COOK TIME:** 15 minutes

NUT-FREE

IT IS IMPORTANT to shred the cheeses yourself for this sauce because the anti-clumping powders used in pre-shredded packaged cheeses prevent the cheese from melting well. High-quality grated Parmesan or Pecorino Romano will work, but avoid the green can and anything that doesn't need to be refrigerated. You can use any combination of cheeses in the same quantities—I chose three of my favorites.

4 tablespoons (½ stick) salted butter

1 tablespoon all-purpose flour

1½ cups heavy (whipping) cream

Dash freshly grated or ground nutmeg

½ cup shredded Asiago cheese

½ cup shredded provolone cheese

½ cup grated Parmesan or Pecorino Romano cheese

Salt

Freshly ground black pepper

1. In a large skillet or sauté pan over low heat, melt the butter. Add the flour and whisk for 2 to 3 minutes, until it is thoroughly mixed with the butter.

2. Pour in the heavy cream and add the nutmeg. Increase the heat to medium and cook, stirring, until the cream starts to simmer. Turn the heat to low and simmer for 2 minutes.

3. Turn off the heat and gradually stir in the Asiago, provolone, and Parmesan cheeses until smooth. Taste and season with salt and pepper.

4. Serve over your favorite pasta, or let cool, transfer to an airtight container, and refrigerate for up to 3 days. This sauce does not freeze well, as it will separate.

ARUGULA AND ALMOND PESTO

MAKES 1 CUP, ENOUGH TO SERVE 4

PREP TIME: 10 minutes

GLUTEN-FREE

FRESH, PEPPERY ARUGULA makes a delicious pesto. There is no need to buy expensive pine nuts for this pesto—dry-roasted unsalted almonds work great, and the skins add a nice color contrast when ground into the sauce. When storing pesto, always cover it completely with a thin layer of oil before refrigerating to prevent the air from turning the pesto brown.

1 cup tightly packed arugula leaves

1 garlic clove, peeled

¼ cup unsalted dry-roasted almonds

½ cup grated Pecorino Romano or Parmesan cheese

½ cup extra-virgin olive oil

Salt

Freshly ground black pepper

1. In a food processor or blender, combine the arugula, garlic, almonds, and Pecorino Romano. With the motor running, slowly drizzle in the oil. Blend for 2 to 3 minutes, until smooth, stopping once to scrape down the sides of the bowl about halfway through. Taste and season with salt and pepper and blend again to combine.

2. Serve over your favorite pasta, or transfer to an airtight container, top with oil to cover, and refrigerate for up to 3 days or freeze for up to 1 month.

Variation tip: Use 1 cup fresh spinach leaves in place of the arugula for a milder flavor.

CREAMY SUN-DRIED TOMATO SAUCE

MAKES 2 CUPS, ENOUGH TO SERVE 4

PREP TIME: 20 minutes | **COOK TIME:** 15 minutes

NUT-FREE

THIS COLORFUL CREAM sauce is a rich topping for any type of ravioli. Use sun-dried tomatoes packed in olive oil for this recipe.

3 tablespoons salted butter

1 small shallot, minced

2 tablespoons all-purpose flour

⅓ cup oil-packed sun-dried tomatoes, thinly sliced

1 cup chicken broth or stock

½ cup heavy (whipping) cream

¼ cup grated Pecorino Romano or Parmesan cheese

2 tablespoons julienned fresh basil leaves (do not use dried)

1 cup fresh baby spinach leaves

Salt

Freshly ground black pepper

1. In a large skillet or sauté pan over low heat, melt the butter. Increase the heat to medium, add the shallot, and sauté for 2 to 3 minutes, until soft.

2. Add the flour and whisk for about 3 minutes, until it is thoroughly mixed with the butter.

3. Stir in the sun-dried tomatoes, broth, heavy cream, and Pecorino Romano. Cook for 3 to 4 minutes, until thickened.

4. Turn off the heat and stir in the basil and spinach. Taste and season with salt and pepper.

5. Serve over your favorite pasta, or let cool, transfer to an airtight container, and refrigerate for up to 3 days. This sauce does not freeze well, as it will separate.

ITALIAN SAUSAGE RAGÙ

MAKES 4 CUPS, ENOUGH TO SERVE 4

PREP TIME: 10 minutes | **COOK TIME:** 1 hour 20 minutes

DAIRY-FREE, GLUTEN-FREE, NUT-FREE

I LEARNED TO make this ragù during my pasta-making education in Bologna with the Tori family of Bluone in Italy Food & Wine Tours. Marcello and Raffaella are truly passionate about Italian food and culture and know a vast network of local chefs, home cooks, food and wine producers, truffle hunters, and more. Their food tours are an authentic experience of Italian life. I started Melina's Fresh Pasta with their support and encouragement.

2 tablespoons extra-virgin olive oil

1 pound sweet Italian sausage, casings removed

1 medium onion, chopped

2 cups red wine

1 (28-ounce) can crushed tomatoes

Salt

Freshly ground black pepper

1. Coat the bottom of a large 4-to-5-quart skillet or sauté pan over medium heat with the oil. Crumble the sausage into the skillet. Cook for 8 to 10 minutes, using a wooden spoon to break up the meat further, until browned.

2. Add the onion and cook for 2 minutes.

3. Pour in the wine and cook for 6 to 10 minutes, until the wine mostly cooks off.

4. Stir in the tomatoes, season with salt and pepper, and bring the sauce to a simmer. Partially cover the skillet and cook for 1 hour, stirring frequently.

5. Serve with your favorite pasta, or let cool, transfer to an airtight container, and refrigerate for up to 3 days or freeze for up to 3 months.

AGNOLOTTI DI MAGRO IN BRODO · 90

MIX-AND-MATCH

Though many filled pasta recipes are based in tradition, there's no reason not to play around with different combinations of dough, fillings, and sauces. Here are some other delicious pairings to try:

DOUGH	FILLING	SHAPE	SAUCE
Whole Wheat Pasta Dough (page 24)	Pork (see Meat Tortellini, page 80)	Tortellini (see page 80)	Roasted Tomato and Thyme Sauce (page 98)
Traditional Egg Pasta Dough (page 20)	Roasted Cauliflower (page 56)	Cappellacci (page 84)	Arugula and Almond Pesto (page 109)
Green pasta dough made with spinach (see 4 Flavored Pasta Doughs, page 28)	Spinach and Artichoke (page 34)	Mezzelune (see page 46)	Sunday Sauce (page 103)
Eggless Pasta Dough (page 22)	Basil Pesto (see page 54)	Ravioli (see page 34 or 42)	Three-Cheese Sauce (page 108)
Gluten-Free Pasta Dough (page 26)	Three Cheese (see Agnolotti di Magro, page 90)	Tortelli (see page 36)	Mushroom Ragù (page 102)
Traditional Egg Pasta Dough (page 20)	Mushroom (page 84)	Raviolone (page 56)	Beef, Red Bell Pepper, and Tomato Sauce (page 107)
Red pasta dough (see 4 Flavored Pasta Doughs, page 28)	'Nduja and Burrata (page 52)	Francobolli (page 64)	Olive oil and grated Parmesan cheese, to taste
Eggless Pasta Dough (page 22)	Pumpkin (page 40)	Tortelloni (page 86)	Sage Butter Sauce (see page 50)
Whole Wheat Pasta Dough (page 24)	"Utica Greens" (page 48)	Lune (page 58)	Fresh Cherry Tomato Sauce (page 106)
Gluten-Free Pasta Dough (page 26)	Crab (page 60)	Pansotti (page 54)	Pesto Cream Sauce (page 101)
Herbed dough made with Italian seasoning (see 4 Flavored Pasta Doughs, page 28)	Fresh Ricotta (page 38)	Triangles (see page 52)	No-Cook Tomato and Castelvetrano Olive Sauce (page 104)

PISTACHIO AND LEMON DOPPIO RAVIOLI · 72

MEASUREMENT CONVERSIONS

	US STANDARD	US STANDARD (OUNCES)	METRIC (APPROXIMATE)
VOLUME EQUIVALENTS (LIQUID)	2 tablespoons	1 fl. oz.	30 mL
	¼ cup	2 fl. oz.	60 mL
	½ cup	4 fl. oz.	120 mL
	1 cup	8 fl. oz.	240 mL
	1½ cups	12 fl. oz.	355 mL
	2 cups or 1 pint	16 fl. oz.	475 mL
	4 cups or 1 quart	32 fl. oz.	1 L
	1 gallon	128 fl. oz.	4 L
VOLUME EQUIVALENTS (DRY)	⅛ teaspoon		0.5 mL
	¼ teaspoon		1 mL
	½ teaspoon		2 mL
	¾ teaspoon		4 mL
	1 teaspoon		5 mL
	1 tablespoon		15 mL
	¼ cup		59 mL
	⅓ cup		79 mL
	½ cup		118 mL
	⅔ cup		156 mL
	¾ cup		177 mL
	1 cup		235 mL
	2 cups or 1 pint		475 mL
	3 cups		700 mL
	4 cups or 1 quart		1 L
	½ gallon		2 L
	1 gallon		4 L
WEIGHT EQUIVALENTS	½ ounce		15 g
	1 ounce		30 g
	2 ounces		60 g
	4 ounces		115 g
	8 ounces		225 g
	12 ounces		340 g
	16 ounces or 1 pound		455 g

	FAHRENHEIT (F)	CELSIUS (C) (APPROXIMATE)
OVEN TEMPERATURES	250°F	120°C
	300°F	150°C
	325°F	165°C
	350°F	180°C
	375°F	190°C
	400°F	200°C
	425°F	220°C
	450°F	230°C

INDEX

Acknowledgments

Thanks to everyone on the Callisto team who made this book possible, with special thanks to my editors, Rachelle Cihonski and Anne Goldberg, for their patience and guidance.

I would like to thank my family for all of their support, especially my parents, Giuseppe and Giuseppa, who came here from Sinopoli, a tiny town in Calabria in southern Italy with my sister, Rita, and brother, Rocco, in tow. My parents' sacrifice to leave all they knew gave us our family with Mike, Julie, and Billy and my awesome nieces and nephews—Angela, Colin, Emily, Sam, Ralph, Marissa, and Joseph—plus our bonus family Tony, Annette, and Lexi Grosso.

Thanks to my Reamer family, Bill and Karen and the rest of the crew, whose support includes everything from taste testing to cookbook promoting to lugging heavy equipment to working in the pasta shop when needed.

A very special thank-you to my husband, Billy, who supports me with love, patience, dishwashing, taste-testing, jokes, and encouragement in everything I do, and who endured two cookbook writing experiences during a pandemic. And also, a small thanks to Simon, the grumbling and stinky basset hound who lays down faithfully behind my legs to try to trip me while I am cooking.

About the Author

Carmella Alvaro, owner, pasta maker, and dishwasher at Melina's Fresh Pasta, in Durham, North Carolina, grew up in an Italian American family originally from Calabria. After years of watching her mother make Italian food with ingredients from her father's garden, she wanted to share in the tradition of cooking from scratch with care and love and serving homemade food to family and friends.

In 2010, she traveled to Bologna, Italy, to learn fresh pasta making. Upon her return home, she started Melina's Fresh Pasta. Since then, the business has grown and now includes a retail shop in Durham, North Carolina, which opened in 2017, offering a greater variety of pastas, sauces, and baked meals to an expanding customer base through farmers' markets, local retailers, farm stands, and home delivery companies. Visit her at MelinasPasta.com.

CPSIA information can be obtained
at www.ICGtesting.com
Printed in the USA
JSHW031944261221
21525JS00004B/5